CONTRAPUNTAL TECHNIQUE IN
THE SIXTEENTH CENTURY

OXFORD
UNIVERSITY PRESS
AMEN HOUSE, E.C. 4
LONDON EDINBURGH GLASGOW
LEIPZIG NEW YORK TORONTO
MELBOURNE CAPETOWN BOMBAY
CALCUTTA MADRAS SHANGHAI
HUMPHREY MILFORD
PUBLISHER TO THE
UNIVERSITY

FIRST EDITION 1922
REPRINTED 1934

CONTRAPUNTAL

TECHNIQUE

IN THE SIXTEENTH CENTURY

BY

R. O. MORRIS

OXFORD
AT THE CLARENDON PRESS

PRINTED IN GREAT BRITAIN AT
THE UNIVERSITY PRESS, OXFORD
BY JOHN JOHNSON
PRINTER TO THE UNIVERSITY

TO

PERCY CARTER BUCK

IN ACKNOWLEDGEMENT OF A DEBT

LONG OUTSTANDING

PREFACE

THE general scope and purport of this volume is set forth in the opening chapter, and this preface need only concern itself with the textual procedure adopted.

First, as to the texts themselves. Where a standard library edition exists—as of Palestrina and Orlando Lasso—this text has of course been followed. The large collections of Proske, van Maldeghem, and Henry Expert are equally familiar to every student of the period, and from each of these I have drawn interesting examples that probably could not have been obtained from any other source. To widen the range of illustration, I have also had recourse to Pedrell's *Hispaniae Scholae Musica Sacra*, Haberl's *Repertorium Musicae Sacrae*, and Barclay Squire's *Ausgewählte Madrigäle*. The editors of these respective volumes need no tribute of mine, for they are all scholars of international repute. But their editions are usually transposed, and for the purposes of this book I have thought it best to retranspose all quotations.

In most of the collections named the editors distinguish accidentals, inserted by them to meet the requirements of *musica ficta*, from those actually written in by the composer, the former being enclosed in a bracket or placed in small print above the note. I have reproduced this distinction where possible—e.g. in the examples taken from Palestrina, Orlando Lasso, and the English composers. In other examples it was not always possible to do so, as the printed texts did not give the necessary indication, and it was manifestly impossible for me to scour the Continent in order to verify every individual sharp and flat in the manuscripts. The accidentals indicated are in every case (in my judgement) such as the composer intended, whether actually inserted by him or not.

I have used only the G and F clefs throughout, with a double G for the tenor, in order to facilitate perusal of the work by non-professional readers who may be interested in the subject.

Regular barring has been adopted throughout, except where some special point was to be illustrated, as in Exx. 38, 39A, and 40A. The tendency of modern editors, I am aware, is all in the other direction, but I cannot agree. These compositions are metrical [1]—as definitely metrical as *Rabbi ben Ezra* or *Locksley Hall*—and the metre should leap to the eye. Regular barring alone can ensure this, and for the true rhythm the reader must trust to his good ear and his good understanding. A fool-proof notation is neither possible nor desirable.

Readers who cannot easily obtain access to the big library editions already mentioned may like to know of some comparatively cheap and popular editions of sixteenth-century music of which they may possess themselves:

(1) Breitkopf & Härtel publish a large collection of masses and motets, edited by Haberl, Bäuerle, and others. Also Barclay Squire's *Ausgewählte Madrigäle*, and Squire & Terry's edition of Byrd's Five-part Mass. These can usually be obtained from Messrs. J. & W. Chester (Department of Ecclesiastical Music).

(2) There is the *Collection Palestrina* (Saint-Gervais), likewise obtainable from Messrs. J. & W. Chester.

(3) There is Dr. Fellowes's wonderful edition of the English Madrigal Composers, published by Stainer & Bell (nineteen volumes so far).

(4) Novello's have done a good deal—Palestrina's *Stabat Mater*, and several of his Masses; masses by Tye, Byrd, and Tallis (all of these have been published in the Octavo Edition, but they are not now all in print). They likewise publish an edition of Tallis's Lamentations (in the *Cathedral Series*, edited by Royle Shore).

---

[1] To prevent possible misconception, let me warn the student against supposing that the measures of this music group themselves into regular periods just as the measures of the poetry group themselves into regular lines. That would be wrong; all that is meant here by 'metrical' is that the harmonic accentuation within each measure is uniform and periodic, not varying unless there is a change of signature. The measures themselves are not grouped in any such regular conformation.

(5) Mention should also be made of the *Downside Motets and Masses* (Cary & Co.); of *Arion*, vols. i and iii (Laudy & Co.); and of the popular edition of Tudor Church Music now in course of issue by the Oxford University Press.

It must be understood that the above editions are not of equal merit; Bäuerle, for instance, halves and even quarters his note values without telling the reader what he has done; so do the editors of the *Collection Palestrina*. The Downside edition retains the original note-values, but halves the measures, and is full of lamentable misprints. But they can all be of service, if used intelligently and with caution. The Fellowes edition, of course, is admirable in every way.

In conclusion, I should like to express my best thanks to Dr. Terry for the loan of his Taverner manuscript scores; to Miss Townsend Warner for the similar loan of manuscript scores by Tye, Whyte, Shepherd, and other of their contemporaries; above all, to Mr. A. H. Fox-Strangways for the unreserved generosity with which he placed the whole of his library at my disposal.

R. O. M.

SYNOPSIS OF CHAPTERS

INDEX OF ILLUSTRATIONS

I

THE POINT OF VIEW

'SINCE the death of these Great Masters', observes Mr. Rockstro,[1] 'it [counterpoint] has undergone no change whatever. No new rules have been, or possibly can be, added to it. It must be taught now—if taught at all—exactly as it was taught in the latter half of the sixteenth century. Our little Treatise, therefore, contains no novelty whatever. The rules it prescribes are those, and those only, to which Palestrina, Vittoria, Luca Marenzio, and the greatest of their contemporaries, yielded their loving obedience.'

A few pages later we come upon the following passage:

'It was the author's original intention to have illustrated the present Treatise entirely with examples selected from the works of the Great Masters . . . But, the difficulty of finding passages exactly adapted to illustrate the precise Rule falling under discussion was so great, that this plan was unavoidably, though very reluctantly, subjected to considerable modification. Abundant quotations have indeed been made from the works of Fux and other famous contrapuntists: but in order to explain his meaning with sufficient clearness to meet the demands of those who are entering upon the study of counterpoint for the first time, the author has found it necessary to write a large number of additional examples, which are distinguished by the sign [given] from those of higher authority.'

At this point, it will be noticed, the logical processes of Mr. Rockstro appear to have suffered an interruption. The 'Rules' he prescribes are those, and those only, to which Palestrina, Vittoria & Co. 'yielded their loving obedience'. These rules, therefore, will naturally be illustrated in every bar that these great composers wrote. Yet, when it comes to the point, we find that Mr. Rockstro has confessedly been unable to find any such illustrations. He has had to write most of them himself; almost the only passage he quotes from a sixteenth-century composer is one from Byrd's *Aspice, Domine*, and on this passage the only comment he finds to make is that 'Byrd has ignored the last clause of Rule LXI at Bars 2, 9, and 17'. Naturally, we feel deeply ashamed that one of our own countrymen should be detected in such licentious

---

[1] *The Rules of Counterpoint*, Introduction, p. 5.

B

behaviour, and we hasten to inquire what the provisions of Rule LXI may be. It is worded as follows:

' . . . A minim placed at the end of a bar, after two crotchets, or a crotchet and two quavers, should always, if possible, be tied to another minim or crotchet, in the beginning of the next bar.'

Passing over the fact that Mr. Rockstro, in his example, has carefully cut Byrd's measures into two, we may remark that exceptions to this rule are somewhat frequent. They are to be found even in Palestrina. In the Mass 'O Admirabile Commercium', for instance, there are fifty-seven of them; at one point—in the Sanctus—nine of them succeed one another with ostentatious rapidity in the space of some twenty measures. And if these things are done in the green tree, what shall be done in the dry? If this is what we find in the blameless Palestrina, what are we to expect from the nefarious Byrd? However, there is no need to insist unduly on this particular rule, for which, as a matter of fact, quite a fair case (though no more) can be made out. It is nevertheless an instance, rather an obvious instance, to show that the 'loving obedience' of which Mr. Rockstro speaks is not always so readily forthcoming as one might have expected. Other rules are even less fortunate, and the impartial observer, who goes all through the list in a spirit of dispassionate inquiry, will begin to understand only too well his perpetual difficulty in finding passages 'exactly adapted to illustrate the precise rule falling under discussion'.

Yet the rules of Mr. Rockstro are not peculiar. They are, more or less, the same as those to be found in almost every text-book of counterpoint. Who invented them, goodness only knows; why they have been perpetuated, it passes the wit of man to explain. Music written to meet their requirements is something altogether *sui generis*, a purely academic by-product,

> Music that never was on sea or land.

What then are we going to do? The rules of counterpoint are found to have no connexion with musical composition as practised in the sixteenth century: are we to abandon the rules, or abandon the sixteenth century? Follow Byrd and Palestrina, or follow Mr. Rockstro and Professor Prout?

The present volume is the writer's answer to this question, so far as it concerns himself. It is, in the main, an exposition of sixteenth-century technique, and, as such, it assumes that that technique is deserving of study. No student worthy the name, however, will be content with assumptions. He will demand reasons. Before devoting his time to counterpoint, he is entitled to ask whether it is likely to prove a profitable study, and what he stands to gain from it.

In the first place, there is the purely historical aspect of the question. Every serious musician should have some knowledge of the history of his art, and of the manner in which his *materia musica* has been accumulated. The sixteenth century is beyond all question one of the great periods of music, and its technique is quite unlike the technique of any succeeding period; it is certainly deserving of study for its own sake, and from no other motive than that of intellectual curiosity. It may be said that to understand and appreciate a particular style it is not necessary to practise it. That is true enough, but it is also true that by actual practice you acquire an inside knowledge that you get in no other way. A student of painting does not regret the time he spends in copying models by Rembrandt or Van Dyck or other great masters of the past, for the insight he thus obtains into their technical aims and methods helps him to appreciate their genius and develop a sense of style, even though his own bent as a painter may lie in quite other directions. Similarly a musician should not hesitate to spend a few months in mastering the idiom of the great sixteenth-century composers, for in doing so he will enlarge his mental horizon, acquire some sense of scholarship, and realize more fully the continuity of musical progress.

But, for the composer at any rate, the study of the sixteenth century has a very real practical as well as a historical interest. Above all, the lesson it has to teach him is that of rhythmical freedom and subtlety. For three hundred years or so we have been slaves of the bar line, and our conception of rhythm has become purely metrical. We learn, probably, to distinguish between 'secondary' rhythm, which places a strong accent at the beginning of each bar and admits a certain variety of figure in between those accents, and 'primary' rhythm which measures out the bars themselves into neat regular groups, usually of two, four, and eight. Having got so far, we stop. Of the wider implications of the term 'rhythm' and of its true nature, we have suffered ourselves to remain in complacent ignorance. Now, at long last, composers are beginning to tire of this monotonous, mechanical sing-song, and to seek a way of escape from it. To the sixteenth century they can turn, not in vain, for guidance. In that period there is no confusion between rhythm and metre. The *rhythmical* accentuation of each part is free, but, independently of the actual rhythmic accents, there is an imaginary *metrical* accentuation which imposes a regular alternation of strong and weak beats to which the harmony of the composition has to conform, although the melody of each voice pursues its own way untrammelled. As soon as a student begins the study of sixteenth-century music, this is the first fact to force itself on his notice; he finds out that in order to write in the idiom of Morley or Orlando Lasso or Vittoria, he has to slough all his old preconceptions, and ask himself, perhaps for the first time, what rhythm really is. This, as was said, is by far the most valuable lesson a composer has to learn, at the moment, from a study of this period. One might add, too, that it is possible to search diligently through all the text-books[1], English and foreign, of the last three hundred years, and never find so much as a hint of it, to put the student on the right track.

It is for this reason, and in no spirit of iconoclasm, that the present writer has found himself compelled to reject *in toto* the traditional methods of instruction, and to indicate an entirely new and, as it seems to him, a more hopeful line of approach. The starting-point has been the conviction that counterpoint, if taught at all, must be taught, as Mr. Rockstro says, exactly as it was taught in the sixteenth century. Hitherto it has not been so taught; even Dr. Kitson (the only authority to betray any real uneasiness) gets no further than to say 'scholastic counterpoint is the adaptation of the principles of Palestrina to modern conditions'. In the process of adaptation, unfortunately, the rhythmic principle—the only principle that really matters—has somehow disappeared; and in any case, is the nineteenth century any less obsolete than the sixteenth? Is it not better to approach the sixteenth century in a spirit of humility, to take it just as we find it, in order to make certain that we know what its principles really were, before we begin to try and adapt them?

It will also be of advantage to the composer to acquire some insight into the workings of the old Modal system. On all sides to-day is heard an outcry against the shackles of the major and minor scale; on all sides we see an inclination to re-examine the problem of musical form, and to reject the view which holds it to be, mainly, the passing from one clearly defined tonality into other related tonalities, and back again. We no longer imagine 'development' to consist in saying in G♭ what you have already said in B♭, and many composers, both by precept and example, betray their belief that tonality, in its present form, is a convention that has outlived its utility. In the sixteenth century the student will see

---

[1] M. Vincent d'Indy's *Cours de composition musicale* is the sole honourable exception of those I have met. Neither Bellermann nor Padre Martini offers any guidance on this point.

the working of rather a different system; and though he will find
here that the system is more closely allied to our own than is
usually admitted, there are certain features of it which he cannot
fail to find suggestive. Here again, however, the text-books fail
him, for most of them carefully evade the question. Mr. Rockstro
is an exception, but once more his disingenuousness—or shall we
call it his excessive ingenuousness?—is too apparent. Rule CXXXV,
'No accidental of any kind must be introduced into any part of the
exercise but the Final Cadence; with the exception of an occasional
B♭ to correct the Tritonus or the False Fifth . . . but even this
can scarcely be tolerated, except in Modes I, II, V, and VI'. Let
the student now turn to the opening chords of Palestrina's *Stabat
Mater* (quoted in Ex. 39) or of *O Bone Jesu* (Ex. 194) and ask
himself how he is to account for them. It is the old story; either
he must scrap Mr. Rockstro or he must scrap Palestrina. One
singles out Mr. Rockstro with reluctance, for he was a pioneer in
the field, and his articles in *Grove's Dictionary* contain much that
is of real value. It is for this very reason that his *Rules of
Counterpoint* cannot be passed over in silence, like similar works
by lesser authorities. What in another is probably ignorance, in
him is sheer dishonesty.

A reform that is needed will inevitably encounter opposition, and
it is most foolish to assume that such opposition is necessarily blind,
perverse, or malicious. There are many teachers of wisdom and
experience to whom this book will not commend itself at first sight.
We grant you, they may say, that the rules of counterpoint need
revision, that in many details they bear no relation to the practice
of the great Polyphonic School of composition, but why cannot they
be simply amended where necessary? Why must you challenge
the entire system? Why cannot you leave us our *Canto Fermo*
and our Five Species?

The answer is, first, that the *Canto Fermo* (in the sense in which
the text-books take it) was, even in those days, an obsolete survival.
When a sixteenth-century composer set to work to compose on
a *Canto Fermo*, he did not spread it out in front of him in a row
of stolid, unappetizing semibreves. He broke it up into fragments,
and treated them thematically with all the rhythmic ingenuity he
could devise. If he used the text-book type of *Canto Fermo* at all,
as he did occasionally (see p. 9, note 1), he did so as a deliberate
archaism. To set such things before the student as the normal,
and indeed the only possible, method of writing counterpoint, is to
paralyse his melodic invention at the outset, and also to give him
an utterly false idea of musical history. As for the Five Species,

it needs a more skilful advocate than the present writer to find any plausible defence for them. They do untold harm by professing to teach the student variety of rhythm, whereas all they really admit is a certain limited variety of rhythmic figure fitted in between regularly recurring metrical accents. They perpetuate the tyranny of the bar line, and do more than anything else to cause that confusion between metre and rhythm from which it is the special mission of counterpoint (rightly understood) to deliver us. Apart from this, all the student can possibly learn from them is the method of employing passing notes, and preparing and resolving the simplest forms of discord, all of which he has already learnt— or should have learnt—from his elementary lessons in harmony. Of course, if counterpoint is frankly taught on this basis; if the teacher says openly to his pupil, ' What we call counterpoint is only elementary harmony. You have already been through it, but we think it is rather fun to put you through it again, and call it by a longer name '—there is candour, at least, in such an attitude. But the pupil's reply is inevitable: ' It may be fun for you. But what do I gain by it ? '

It must not be thought that the method of instruction implied in the sequence of chapters in this volume involves or permits any relaxation of discipline. The student who embarks on it in any such belief will be rudely disappointed. He will find that where he was formerly chastised with whips, he is now chastised with scorpions. It is much easier to write like Cherubini than to write like Byrd; it requires far less exertion to produce a ream of scholastic counterpoint than a single page in the vein of Mr. Thomas Morley. These remarks are not intended for a moment to discourage the learner. They are just a kindly warning, that he may not suspect us of any amiable desire to cast authority to the winds. From arbitrary rules, claiming a sanctity to which they have no right, he is entitled to be free, but there are plenty of genuine rules ready to take their place. And if he is wise, he will not be content to know, in theory, that their ultimate sanction rests in the practice of Tallis and Byrd, of Lasso and Palestrina. He will begin by frequenting the precincts of Westminster Cathedral, or any other place where this music is habitually sung. He will then have a knowledge of counterpoint which no book can impart, for he will have begun to realize its beauty.

THE MODAL SYSTEM

I. Every student knows that if you take the diatonic series of notes represented by the white keys of the pianoforte, the sequence of notes lying between C and c (or any of their octaves) constitutes what we call the major scale. It may not have occurred to him that it is possible to start also on any other notes of the series, and that the notes from E to e say, or G to g, will give other scales, similar to the major scale, and yet differing from it, and from each other; similar, in that they all consist of five tones and two semitones; differing, in that the order of the tones and semitones varies with each respective scale. In the C scale, for instance, the order is TTSTTTS; in the E scale it is STTTSTT. You are working on the same diatonic series, but by selecting another note as your starting and finishing point, you envisage a new aspect or 'mode' of that series. How many such modes can you have? Clearly, seven, for after the seventh, whether ascending or descending, you reach the octave, and your next series would be merely a repetition of the first. The modal system, however, recognized a further set of distinctions, based not on the order of the tones and semitones, but on the compass of the melody. If a melody in any given mode lay between the final of that mode and its octave, the mode was said to be in its Authentic form; if it lay between the dominant of the mode and its octave, it was said to be in its Plagal form. (Plagal and Authentic melodies alike, of course, had to end on the final of the mode: e.g. the *compass* of the Dorian [Authentic] mode, D—d, is the same as that of the Hypomixolydian [Plagal] mode; but the last note of a Dorian melody must be D, whereas that of a Hypomixolydian must be G.)

There were thus in all fourteen theoretically possible modes, seven Authentic, and seven Plagal. Ex. 1 will show exactly what they were, what names were given to them,[1] and which notes

---

[1] These names were borrowed from the modal system of the ancient Greeks, but it must not be imagined that the Greek system and the ecclesiastical system were identical. To enter into the difference here would merely befog the student, who would be well advised not to trouble his head about Greek music, unless he intends to make it a special branch of study.

served as the dominant and mediant respectively in each mode.
For the time being, the student should notice:

1. That the eleventh and twelfth modes are purely theoretical, the imperfection of the fifth and the redundancy of the fourth (B–F, F–B) making the series quite unusable, both in Plagal and Authentic forms.

2. That the dominant of the third mode is C, not B, although the compass of the corresponding Plagal mode is B–b. The reason is that although B was the original dominant of the mode (as you would expect, the dominant being normally a fourth below the final), C was eventually substituted for it. It was found, probably, that B, being a constituent of the forbidden tritone F–B, was not fitted to serve as the most prominent note (after the final) of the mode.

3. That (possibly for the same reason) the mediant of the seventh mode (and the dominant of the eighth) is C and not B. The mediant of an Authentic mode always serves as the dominant of the corresponding Plagal mode, except that in the fourth mode the dominant is A and not G.

The distinction between Authentic and Plagal can easily be illustrated from English folk-song. 'Bold Young Farmer', for instance, is Authentic (Mixolydian); 'Trees they do grow high' is Plagal (Hypodorian).

It should be here stated that this theory of fourteen possible and twelve actual modes did not pass unchallenged. It was first formulated by Glareanus in a work entitled *Dodecachordon*, and published in 1547. Earlier theory recognized eight modes only, i.e. the series starting on D, E, F, and G respectively, with their corresponding Plagal forms; and conservative writers still preferred, even in much later times, to adhere to the old ecclesiastical tradition of eight modes. When we have seen the modifications which, in practice, crept into the modal system, we shall see that the difference is one of doctrine rather than of reality. These modifications we must now consider.

II. First of all, it may already have occurred to the student that the distinction between Authentic and Plagal, valid enough from a purely melodic point of view, must necessarily be difficult, if not impossible, to maintain in polyphonic composition for mixed voices. The natural compass of a bass, for instance, as compared with that of a tenor, is about a fifth below; similarly with the relationship of alto to tenor, and of treble to alto. Therefore, if you are writing in a mode whose Authentic compass suits a tenor voice, it will be the corresponding Plagal compass that will lie most naturally for the bass, and so on. And if you turn to the composition of the period to see what happens, you find this is actually the case: in four-part composition for mixed voices, two parts keep generally to the Authentic compass, two to the Plagal. If the tenor and treble are Authentic, the alto and the bass will be Plagal, and vice versa. How then, it may well be asked, can you speak of a composition as being in any given mode when, if half of it is in one mode, the other half is admittedly in another?

The answer is that such descriptions are purely conventional, and the convention governing them is that the compass of the tenor part is the determining factor. If that is Authentic, the whole composition is considered as Authentic; if Plagal, as Plagal. This convention is, of course, a survival from earlier times, when all composition was based on a plain-song melody sung by the tenor, the other parts singing round it in *faux-bourdon* or some other form of discant. By the sixteenth century, however, this strict writing on a *Canto Fermo* had been superseded by other methods;[1] a composer was free to invent his own themes if he wished, and if he used a plain-song melody (as he still very frequently did), he would employ it, as a rule, thematically, i.e. break it up into its component phrases, and devise rhythmical variants of these for fugal treatment (see Chap. VII). But the tenor continued to dictate the name of the mode to the whole composition; quite irrationally, for the tenor did not necessarily end on the final of the mode, which can only be determined for certain by looking at the last note of the bass. It is the bass which gives you the final of the mode in which a composition is written; the tenor which decides as to whether the form of that mode is to be considered as Authentic or as Plagal.

III. While we are touching this point, it may be as well to mention also that all the modes could be taken in a transposed position a fifth below their normal range, with a B♭ in the signature to indicate such transposition.[2] In this case, of course, the final note of the bass must be restored to its untransposed position in order to declare the mode. If the bass ends, for instance, on G, and there is a B♭ in the signature, the true final is D, and the com-

---

[1] It was still employed occasionally, however, much as composers to-day still write every now and again upon a ground bass. Instances of the use of a strict *Canto Fermo* in semibreves can be found in Byrd's *Cantiones Sacrae* (1589 series, Nos. 18 and 19); in Orlando Lasso's *Sixth Penitential Psalm*; in Aichinger's *Antiphonae super Psalmos,* and elsewhere. In all of these, though, the *Canto Fermo* is given impartially to other voices besides the tenor.

[2] But the accidental A♭ must not be employed in the transposed form of a mode although E♭ can be used freely in the untransposed form.

position is either in the Dorian or the Hypodorian mode, transposed. Any other form of transposition in the ecclesiastical music
of the period is extremely rare, though in secular music, as we shall
see, there was less orthodoxy. Modern editors, however, transpose
these old works freely to whatever pitch they think best adapted
to the needs of a modern choir. There is no theoretical difficulty
about this whatsoever; by putting, for instance, five flats in your
signature, you can get the Dorian series (starting on E♭), the
Phrygian (starting on F), the Lydian (starting on G♭), and so on;
similarly with any other number, either of sharps or flats, in the
signature. The differentiation between one mode and another
depends not on any absolute difference of pitch, but on the relative
disposition of the tonic and semitonic intervals. No doubt the
singers of the sixteenth century could have sung their melodies
at any pitch, for they were taught by the sol-fa methods;[1] but
as a matter of notation, only the one form of transposition was in
use, indicated, as was said, by a single flat in the signature (B♭,
transposing everything a fifth down or a fourth up, as the case
might be).

IV. The next modifications to be discussed are those permitted,
or rather, necessitated, by the laws of what is known as *Musica
Ficta*. To learn what this means, we can do no better than take
the definition given us by the author of the treatise *Ars contra-
puncti* :[2] 'Music is called Ficta when we make a tone to be a semitone, and conversely a semitone to be a tone. For every tone is
divisible into two semitones, and consequently the semitonic signs
can appear between all tones.' In other words, *Musica Ficta* means,
as we should say, chromatic alteration. It was called 'Ficta'
because for a long time such alterations did not appear in the
written music. Ecclesiastical tradition required that, in appearance
at least, the diatonic integrity of the modes should be respected,
and the chromatic alterations were left to the discretion of the
singers, who were expected to introduce them in performance, in
accordance with certain more or less clearly understood rules.

It must here be frankly stated that there is, and always will be,
a certain difference of opinion as to the exact interpretation of these
rules. The earlier theoretical writers do not always express themselves clearly on the subject, and one cannot turn to the actual
compositions for enlightenment, for the simple reason that (as above
stated) the alterations were not at first permitted[3] to appear in the

---

[1] Ancestor of our own Tonic Sol-fa. See *Oxford History of Music*, vol. ii, pp. 72–81.

[2] Coussemaker, *Scriptores*, iii, 23. Quoted by Wooldridge, op. cit.

[3] And long after this prejudice had disappeared, the custom itself remained.

music. There is evidence that the scope of *Musica Ficta* varied at different periods and (probably) in different localities; with highly trained singers it became doubtless a matter of instinct rather than a mechanical application of definite formulae. To investigate such a matter in detail is the task of the historian. It is beyond the scope of this treatise, and the following rules must be taken for general guidance only. The subject does not admit of dogmatic ruling; at the same time, the student who observes these rules cannot go very far astray, and he had much better adhere to them rigorously until he is experienced enough to use his own discretion.

1. The tritone and its correlative, the diminished fifth, are forbidden intervals, both in melody and harmony. It was the necessity for correcting these intervals that first gave rise to *Musica Ficta*, B♭ always being sung instead of B♮ where necessary for this purpose.

2. It was soon recognized that this purpose could as well be effected by sharpening the F as by flattening the B.

3. The convenience of being able to alter the remaining intervals of the scale (D–E, G–A, C–D) in a similar manner could not be overlooked, and the chromatic notes necessary for this purpose, E♭, G♯, C♯, also came into general use.

4. These five chromatic notes, B♭, E♭, F♯, C♯, G♯, are the only chromatic notes permitted in the strict modal system of the sixteenth century. *They are not to be taken as the enharmonic equivalents of* A♯, D♯, G♭, D♭, *and* A♭. These latter made their appearance tentatively in some of the earlier secular music, but they are not used with any freedom until the close of the period, by which time the madrigal writers had virtually ceased to pay even a nominal respect to modal propriety.

5. The most important use of chromatic alteration, apart from the perfecting of the tritone, is in the formation of the cadence. This is explained and illustrated in the next section of this chapter.

6. Where a melody rises or falls by a tone, and then falls or rises by the same interval, the *tendency* is to reduce the tone to a semitone by chromatic alteration when possible. E. g. the progression A G A would often be sung A G♯ A, A B A as A B♭ A (but never, e. g., B A♯ B or C D♭ C, because A♯ and

Chromatic alteration was largely taken for granted throughout the Polyphonic period, the accidentals inserted in the music being, as a rule, only those which the singers could not be trusted to introduce at their own discretion.

D♭, as already explained, do not yet exist). But it must be emphasized that this is only a tendency; its indiscriminate application as a rule would have disastrous results. The student, when he has occasion to use such progressions in his own writing, should consider each case on its own merits. The beauty of the opening phrase of *Veni, Sponsa Christi*, for instance (see Ex. 192), would be utterly ruined if the E were sung as E♭. On the other hand, in the cadence from *Sacerdotes Domini* (Ex. 24♮) it is precisely the logical application of this rule, causing the F♮ of the alto to be answered by the F♯ of the treble, that gives the cadence its extraordinary fascination.

V. We must now consider the type of cadence used in the modal writing of the sixteenth century. 'Cadence' in its derivative sense, of course, means simply 'fall', and the cadence of a plain-song melody was formed, as a rule, by descending, or 'falling' one degree to its final. It is in this sense that Shakespeare says:

> That strain again, it had a dying fall.

One of the first problems harmony had to solve was the accompaniment of this melodic procedure by the other voice or voices. After various experiments it was found that the most natural and satisfying method in two-part writing was for the accompanying voice to ascend to the final by a semitone. This could be done either above or below; in the former case, the final chord would be that of the octave, the penultimate that of the major sixth; in the latter, the final chord would be the unison, the penultimate that of the minor third (Exx. 2 and 3 illustrate this in its simplest form). In three-part writing, it was found that while the two upper parts were engaged in the manner just described the best thing the bass [1] could do was to ascend to the final by a fourth or drop to it by a fifth (Exx. 4 and 5). If the cadence itself was in the bass, one of the upper parts rose by a semitone to the octave, the other either rose by a tone to the fifth or fell by a semitone to the third (Exx. 6 and 7). In writing for four or more parts, the cadence is simply a variety of one of these forms, with one or more notes doubled (Exx. 8 to 14).

Thanks to the aid of *Musica Ficta*, as described in the last section, these cadences can be formed on any degree of any mode, except E and B. Before explaining the treatment of these degrees, one or two further remarks must be added about the normal cadence.

---

[1] By 'bass' is meant here the lowest of the parts employed at the moment. The 'acting bass', so to speak.

(*a*) It will be noticed in the above examples the final chord is not invariably, as we should say, complete. Even in four-part writing the sixteenth-century masters often preferred to omit the third from their final chord.

(*b*) When the third is present in the final chord, it is usually made major by the help of *Musica Ficta,* no matter on what degree of the mode it occurs. In the final cadence this is invariably the case, and so also in any important cadence that marks the end of a clearly-defined musical section. Elsewhere it is at the option of the writer to sharpen the third if it is naturally minor, *but not to flatten it if it is naturally major.*

(*c*) The examples of cadence already given show the harmonic skeleton in its simplest form. In practice, cadence is usually treated 'in binding manner'; i.e. single or double suspensions are introduced, whose resolutions may be plain or (within certain clearly defined limits) ornamental. The treatment of suspended discords is explained in Chapter V, but meantime a glance at Exx. 15 to 23 will give the student some idea of the preparation and formation of cadence in the composition of the period.

(*d*) In composition for three or more parts, when the bass proceeds to the final by the rise of a fourth or fall of a fifth, the tenor, instead of falling a tone to the final, may rise a tone to the third. In the cadence at the end of a composition (or one of the main sections of the Mass), the tenor almost always does one of these two things (except in a Plagal cadence which will be considered later). But in an intermediate cadence the spacing of the parts may be quite different. Exx. 24 and 25 will make this plainer than any verbal explanation could do.

The student will already have realized that this uniformity of cadential treatment, together with the other alterations permitted by *Musica Ficta,* tends to obliterate very largely the distinction between one mode and another. This is the second of the important modifications mentioned on page 8. First the distinction between Authentic and Plagal went by the board, so that our twelve possible modes (the B modes being impossible in any case) are reduced to six. Secondly, by the constant substitution of B♭ for B, the Dorian and Lydian modes became virtually transposed forms of the Aeolian and Ionian respectively, so that really we have only four modes instead of six. Moreover, the Mixolydian (G) mode, thanks to the sharpening of the F at the cadence, lost a good deal of its personality, and tended to merge into the Ionian, though its capitulation was not so abject as that of the Lydian, whose B♭ actually appeared in the signature.

Theory was thus quite justified in recognizing eight modes only (i. e. four Authentic modes, with their corresponding Plagal forms). It was illogical, however, to admit the Dorian and Lydian modes, and to exclude the Aeolian and Ionian. In reality it was the two former modes that were absorbed into the latter, and not vice versa.

The E mode (the Phrygian) remained distinct from the others, because it did not admit of a perfect cadence, as the note D♯ did not exist. The Phrygian cadence was formed by the bass, or lowest part, descending to the final by a semitone, whilst the upper part ascended by a tone to the octave above. In three-part writing, the motion of the additional part was from A to G♯, the chordal progression being thus F A D—E G♯ E. In four-part writing and upwards, the A or the D (or both) could be doubled in the penultimate chord, and the final chord completed by the addition of the B (Exx. 26 to 31). But as this cadence is in itself of a somewhat inconclusive character, it was often reinforced at the end of a composition by a Plagal cadence (i.e. one in which the final chord is preceded by the chord on the fifth below the final; in this case on A. If the student likes for convenience to think of this as a subdominant progression, well and good; but he must remember that this is modern terminology, and that, as a matter of fact, A is the *Dominant* of the Hypophrygian mode). Very often the Plagal cadence alone is used, especially in Palestrina, who employs the true 'Phrygian' cadence very sparingly. The 'Phrygian' cadence, however, is often used as an intermediate cadence for the sake of variety in compositions that are not in the Phrygian mode; it can be formed in this way on D and A as well as on E.

The Plagal cadence may also be used freely in all the other modes as well as the Phrygian (Exx. 32 to 34). It is in itself less directly conclusive in character than the perfect cadence, and to use it effectively both care and judgement are required. Until the student is certain of his ability to handle it properly, he may be wise to prepare the way for it by a full close, following this up with a Plagal cadence as reinforcement (as illustrated by Ex. 35 from a motet by Vittoria, who has a special fondness for this device).

The 'interrupted' cadence is used as freely in the music of the sixteenth century as in music of the harmonic period. No recipe can be given for its employment; it is a matter of musical instinct. Two points, however, are worth mentioning:

1. It is particularly effective in fugal writing, when the 'interruption' is caused by the thematic progression of the bass (Ex. 36).

2. In the music of this period, the progression instead of being
    upwards from dominant to 'submediant' is often down-
    wards to 'subdominant', both words being used in their
    modern sense (Ex. 37).

It remains to explain what is meant by 'modulation' at this
period, and what range of modulation is permitted in each given
mode. Modulation means, in a word, cadence. When you hear,
for instance, of a 'modulation to G' occurring in a composition in
the Phrygian mode, it does not mean that the harmonic centre of
gravity has shifted from the tonality of E to that of G. Such con-
ceptions are quite foreign to the writers of the sixteenth century;
what is meant is simply that a cadence has been formed (in one of
the ways above described) on the note G, in a position where its
cadential character is unmistakably felt. The usual tables of
'regular and conceded modulations' commonly given, refer only to
plain-song; in polyphonic music the range of modulation permitted
in each mode is, in practice, rather more restricted. The following
list has been arrived at empirically by the present writer; no
separate list is given for the Plagal modes, as it is extremely
doubtful whether, from the point of view of modulation, any absolute distinction between the Plagal and Authentic forms can be
established.[1]

Dorian	D A F, and more sparingly, G, C.
Phrygian	E A G, „ „ „ C, D.
Lydian	F A C, „ „ „ D.
Mixolydian	G D C, „ „ „ A & F.
Aeolian	A E C, „ „ „ D, G.
Ionian	C G A, „ „ „ D, F.

It must be observed that Padre Martini (a very great authority)
forbids modulation on the second and seventh degrees of any mode
as being 'troppo irregulare' and 'alienissima dal Tuono' (*Saggia
di Contrapunto*, parte prima, p. 26, note). This rule is so frequently
infringed that it cannot be taken as absolute. See, for instance,
the reiterated close on D at the words 'et propter nostram salutem
descendit de coelis' in the Credo of Palestrina's *Missa Papae
Marcelli*, which is in the C mode. In the same composer's hymn,

---

[1] Mr. Wooldridge's table (given in the *Oxford History*, vol. ii, pp. 200, 201) suggests
that he had come to a similar conclusion, although his list does not agree in every
detail with that here given. But in a series of articles by the same writer which
appeared in the *Musical Antiquary* in 1912–13, the Plagal and Authentic modulations
are not always given as identical. Evidently Mr. Wooldridge (like myself) found
some difficulty in arriving at a final conclusion.

Tantum Ergo, which is in the E mode, there are two clearly marked closes on D. Similar instances are not hard to find.

No cadence is ever formed on the note B, because (owing to the non-existence of D♯), it cannot be made the basis of a major triad. Even the 'Plagal' and 'Phrygian' cadences are therefore *impossible*; the perfect cadence more obviously so, because not only the final chord but the penultimate chord as well (which would require the note A♯) cannot be formed.

III

RHYTHM

It has already been observed (see p. 3) that in the polyphonic music of the sixteenth century a double system of accentuation is employed. The rhythmical accentuation of each individual part is free, that is to say, the accents do not occur at strictly regular intervals, whereas the composition as a whole does conform to a fixed metrical scheme in which strong and weak accents succeed one another in a pre-determined order. This idea may seem difficult to grasp at first, but the student who gives it a few moments' consideration will find that it is not really so unfamiliar as he may think. In the rhythm of poetry there is a precisely similar duality, as any one may quickly convince himself. Take the familiar opening of Milton's *Paradise Lost*:

> Of Man's first disobedience, and the fruit
> Of that forbidden tree, whose mortal taste
> Brought death into the world, and all our woe,
> Sing, Heavenly Muse . . . .

There is no doubt as to the metre of this; it is the common five-foot iambic metre which is scanned thus:

$$\cup - \mid \cup - \mid \cup - \mid \cup - \mid \cup -.$$

but only a very ignorant person would accentuate the lines in this manner when reading them:

> Ŏf Mān's′ fīrst dĭs′ŏbē′diĕnce ānd′ thĕ frūit′
>
> Ŏf thāt′ fŏrbīd′dĕn trēe′ whŏse mōr′tăl tāste,

and so on. This would be the merest sing-song, in which the metrical accents are falsely emphasized at the expense of the natural rhythm and stress of the words. The latter must be preserved, for it enables us to distinguish between the more and the less important elements of the thought which the words convey. Yet the metrical scheme also persists. You may not hear it, but it is somewhere in the back of your head all the time, as a kind of pattern or standard to which every line of the poetry is referred, more or less unconsciously, for comparison. And the delight of reading good verse arises largely from this duality of apprehension.

Each verse as it comes is both true to itself and true to type; the ear catches the stress in all its variety, the mind retains its hold on the quantities, short and long, short and long, in orderly recurrence. Between the rhythmical accent (the accent of stress) and the metrical accent (the accent of quantity) there is a continual interplay; sometimes they coincide, sometimes they are at odds, and the rhythmical problem before the poet is to strike the just balance. Too much coincidence means monotony; too much at-oddness means chaos.

Now, once it is realized that a double system of accentuation is habitually employed and recognized in poetry, there is no difficulty in applying a similar conception to music. The only thing that may stand in the student's way is the custom of the bar-line, which he has come to regard as necessarily indicating a strong rhythmic accent. It will be shown later that the bar-line (inserted in modern editions of sixteenth-century music for convenience to the eye, and to mark the beginning of each measure) has a purely metrical significance, and exercises no control whatever over the rhythmical accent. Meantime, before proceeding to demonstrate this by example, it is, perhaps, advisable to discuss rather more fully the difference between stress accent and quantity accent.

In most languages the mathematical distinction between long and short (one long = two shorts) is largely theoretical, a convention observed only for metrical purposes. In practice, a long syllable is more or less long, a short more or less short, according to the amount of stress it receives in utterance; in our own language, for instance, very many syllables are potentially short or long, and it is only when you see them in a particular context, and can judge (by the sense of the words) whether they are stressed or unstressed, that you can classify them as short or long. In other words, quantity is dominated, and often actually determined, by stress. In music, on the other hand, quantitative relationships are mathematically exact. A semibreve is always equal to two minims, and a dotted semibreve to three, and so on, and even if a composer likes to complicate matters by writing five crotchets to be played in the space of a semibreve, or five quavers in that of a dotted crotchet, the new relationship can still be stated in mathematical terms, $\frac{5}{2}$ or $\frac{5}{3}$, or whatever the ratio may be. The performance of concerted music is only made possible by the strict observance of these time-proportions. Consequently, every note has to receive its just value, and if that value is longer than the values of the notes in the immediate vicinity, it tends to assert itself over them and to make itself felt as the accentual centre of the group. Let me try to make this clear by an example (Ex. 38). Here you have no time-signature, no metrical indication of any kind to prejudice you, no text to show you where a stress might be required by the sense of the words. Suppose you try to articulate the passage. It is obvious that to split it up into regular groups of three or regular groups of four is impossible, save by an act of sheer violence. Try as you may, you will not be able to feel that the main accents fall in any other places than the ones marked, for the simple reason that at each of these places there is a momentary arresting of the rhythmic flow, which catches your attention and keeps it in suspense for an instant until the flow is resumed. That instant is quite enough to make you conscious that an accent has been created, without the aid of any dynamic increase. So strongly, indeed, is the force of the 'agogic' accent felt that it may almost be said to carry its own stress with it, making the listener imagine it has been reinforced by stress, when as a matter of fact it has not been so reinforced. Had the notes in the example above been of equal duration, the tendency would have been to hear them mentally as regular groups of two, three, or four notes, with an imaginary stress on the first note of each group. Here one does not, cannot do that, because the varying magnitude of the notes affords an actual basis of differentiation which the ear cannot ignore.

Now it is important to bear this principle in mind. The reader, finding that the bar-line gives him no clue to the position of the rhythmical accents, will naturally want to know how he is to find out where those accents are. In the music of the sixteenth century there are no stress marks and *sforzandos*, as there are in modern music. There are the words, certainly, and where they indicate (as they often do) the accentuation of the music to which they are set, there is of course no difficulty. But in many places they give no such indication; notably in certain movements of the Mass, where the composer does not fit the music syllable by syllable to the text, but writes the music simply as music, inserting at the beginning of the piece the text to which it is fitted, and leaving the copyist or the singer (as the case may be) to accommodate the syllables of the text to their appropriate musical phrase. To articulate such passages, the student must find out where the accents of duration are most strongly felt, and in the preceding paragraph he has been given a principle on which to look for them. That principle may be expressed briefly thus, that a note which is either preceded or followed (and still more strongly, one that is both preceded *and* followed) by notes of smaller value than itself tends to have the force of an accent. In the example already given, there was no

c 2

ambiguity; but melodies are not always so obliging. The student may often find himself in doubt, and he will do well to bear the following maxims in mind:

1. Accents should be neither too many nor too few. There must be enough of them to hold the melody firmly together and prevent it, so to speak, from sagging, but they should not be so close together as to detract from each other's importance.

2. The rhythm of a phrase is frequently (some would say 'always') anacrusic; that is to say, the accented note is not necessarily the first note of the phrase, but may be preceded by an unaccented note or series of notes—an 'up-beat' as we should call it to-day.

Even so, there will be many doubtful cases, and a rhythmical analysis of the same passage by different hands is quite likely to show some divergence in detail. That does not matter in the least. It is largely a matter of discretion and common sense; the important thing is to have some method whereby you can apprehend a melody as a rhythmical organism, built up of clearly defined accentual groups, and not as a haphazard series of unrelated sounds. If the student happens to find a passage that is quite unamenable to analysis by the methods here suggested, he is justified in regarding it as a case of *dormitat Homerus*—a momentary lapse of technique. He should always test the rhythmical structure of his own counterpoint in this manner; a properly constructed melody will convey to the ear just the same sense of freedom and balance as the prose composition of a good writer. You can always tell when a piece of prose sounds unrhythmic, and when you come to analyse it, you generally find its failure due to one of three causes:

1. The stresses are too many, the result being a feeling of hurry and congestion.

2. They are too few, which gives an impression of flabbiness and want of vigour.

3. They are too regular in their occurrence, in which case you feel a lack of freedom, just as in cases (1) and (2) you feel a lack of balance.

In music, in precisely the same manner, a melodic period will be felt as rhythmic or unrhythmic in so far as the distribution of the accents complies with this twofold artistic requirement—freedom and balance.

It has already been said more than once that the time-signature at the beginning of a sixteenth-century composition is of purely metrical significance, exercising an important influence on the harmonic structure of the composition, but having nothing to do with the rhythmical structure of the parts taken individually. It now remains to prove that this is true. The harmonic aspect of the question is discussed in Chapter V; for the moment, it is the rhythm of the single voices that we have to consider. Our first two examples are very well known; they are both from Palestrina's *Stabat Mater*. Examples 39 and 40 show them barred out at regular intervals in accordance with the time-signature, and it can be seen at once that to attempt to place a strong accent at the beginning of every such group is to make nonsense of the words; for instance:

$$> \cup \cup > \quad \cup \cup >$$
Fac ut tecum lugeam

$$\cup \quad \cup > \cup \cup > > >$$
fac ut ardeat cor meum

$$\cup \cup > \cup \quad > \quad \cup \cup$$
In amando Christum Deum.

The above is clearly gibberish. In Examples 39 A and 40 A we have the same two excerpts barred out in accordance with the real rhythmic accentuation: in this case, however, to save space, the top line of the music only is given. It will be noticed that in both cases the scansion—that is to say, the size and conformation of the rhythmical groups—is irregular, and designedly so, the intention being, as we shall see, to bring out the *rhythm* of the words and not merely to reproduce their metre. Furthermore, this principle is observed whatever the time-signature may be (in Example 39, for instance, the signature is duple ($\frac{4}{2}$), in Example 40 triple ($\frac{3}{1}$).

It remains for the student to satisfy himself that such cases as this are normal, and not exceptional. To do so, he must study the scores of the period in detail, but a few more examples are appended which have been purposely chosen to show that the principle enunciated is not confined to any one country, language, or school of composition. In these examples the imaginary metrical divisions are shown by the bar-line, while the stress marks indicate the real rhythmical accentuation. It must be remembered that the stress marks do not indicate anything in the nature of a violent *sforzando*, but are there merely to show that the rhythmic accents do not necessarily coincide with the metrical accents. No. 41 is from Morales (Spain), No. 42 from Orlando Lasso (Flemish, but at that time resident in Munich), No. 43 from Byrd (England), No. 44 from Morley (England), No. 45 from Bertani [1] (Italy).

It is also worth noticing, that in secular composition (madrigals, canzonets, and so on) the principle of irregular accentuation is not so systematically followed as in the great sacred forms of music, the

[1] Quoted in *Arion*, vol. i.

Mass and the Motet. Frequently you will come across melodic sentences which resolve naturally into regular units of duple or triple measure; but the interesting thing to note here is that such measure is frequently not the measure indicated by the time-signature of the composition. If the former is duple, the latter is often triple, and vice versa. Examples 46 and 47 (both from Morley) illustrate this clearly. Examples 48 and 49 (both from André Pevernage) illustrate the further point that a rhythmic group of 8 units need not subdivide geometrically into two fours or four twos; in both these passages the unit of 8 divides arithmetically (*a*) into 6 + 2, (*b*) into 3 + 5, and in the second of them the rhythmical groups of 8 do not coincide at all with the metrical divisions.

From now onward, then, it will be taken as clear that the measure or time-signature of any polyphonic composition of this period, sacred or secular, does not exercise any control whatever over the rhythmical structure of any of the individual parts.

It was remarked above that the words of the text often indicate the rhythmical outline of the music. While this is true in a general sense, it must be observed that a composer is nevertheless free to a considerable extent to settle the details of his rhythm in accordance with his own purely musical requirements. The examples already quoted from the *Stabat Mater* are worth considering rather more closely from this point of view. It is obvious that Palestrina could equally well have set these lines without telescoping the measures, as he actually does. (Exx. 50 and 51, for instance, are also quite a fair musical equivalent of the verbal rhythm.) To the question, why did he not so set them? the only answer can be that he preferred it otherwise; that even in setting a metrical text (this hymn is in the trochaic four-foot, $- \cup | - \cup | - \cup | - \cup$) he deliberately chose an irregular musical accentuation, as giving greater freedom and flexibility without in any way distorting or violating the rhythm of the words. How skilfully he reconciles the two can be realized by examining the first instance in detail. Here the second syllable of *Stabat* is unimportant, but from its position before another consonant—and particularly the consonant m—it acquires a certain quantitative value. The composer is therefore at liberty to dwell on it to some extent, and as a matter of fact he gives it the value of a semibreve. But he is careful to put this semibreve in between two other notes of equal value, so that it is not made unduly prominent. In the third measure, on the other hand, the third syllable of *dolorosa*—clearly the accentual climax of the line—also receives the value of a semibreve and no more; but in this case the semibreve follows a note of only half its own value, so that the ear will more easily recognize its accentual force. A slight increase in dynamic stress—for which the choirmaster can be trusted—is all that is needed to make its rhythmical importance unmistakable. It will not be a waste of time for the student to examine some of the remaining examples by himself, considering carefully in each case (1) whether the composer could have found other rhythmical equivalents for the given texts, and (2) if so, whether there is any evident reason why he should have given this particular one the preference.

In the examples so far given the text has clearly indicated to some extent the rhythmical outline of the music. To supplement these, one or two examples from settings of the Mass are appended to show the student how the same ideal of freedom and balance is aimed at by the composer when there is no verbal rhythm to influence him. In articulating these passages the only principle to guide us is the one already enunciated, viz., that any momentary reduction in the rate of the rhythmic flow tends to create an accent, and that such an accent, though strictly speaking an accent of duration only, tends to carry its own stress with it. Applying this principle, we find once more that the accents occur irregularly, and that the rhythmical groups or units defined by them are correspondingly irregular in size. That is just what we should have expected, having found already that in sacred music (even to metrical words) this same freedom, this irregularity which never degenerates into confusion, is the rhythmical ideal to which the composer aspires.

But the composers of the sixteenth century were not content with the effect obtainable by contrasting the real rhythmical accent with the imaginary metrical accent. Above all, they loved to make the rhythmical accents of each part cross and clash with those of every other part. This constant rhythmical conflict is the most vital and suggestive feature in the whole of the sixteenth-century technique, and the one which the student should above all endeavour to imitate in his own counterpoint exercises. He may find it hard at first, for it is a real technical discipline, but this need cause him no discouragement. The difficulty is largely one of preconception, of realizing that the bar-line is not really the tyrant we have come to imagine it. As soon as the student is able to convince himself of his new-found liberty, he will feel nothing but delight at being free to construct his rhythms in accordance with his own artistic instinct. He will not regret his crutches as soon as he finds out that he is not really a cripple.

A few examples have been chosen to illustrate this device, and more will be found in Chapter VIII, for it is an aspect of technique to which the English composers paid special attention, and many of them, Byrd and Morley in particular, exhibit an extraordinary daring and resourcefulness. It will now be clear why we have examined at such length the principles of rhythmical articulation governing a single line of melody. It was necessary in order that when we came to illustrate the varieties of rhythmic combination which distinguish the music of this period from all the music of a later date, the student could feel himself on sufficiently firm ground to understand the method of procedure, and not be compelled to ask at every turn, ' How do you arrive at this? Why do you scan this part in such and such a manner, and this other part quite differently?' All we have to do now is to leave the examples to speak for themselves, and to assure the reader that though they have been chosen specially to illustrate this aspect of the technique, they are in no sense abnormal. The method they illustrate is the rule, and not the exception, as any one may satisfy himself who will be at the pains to carry out further analysis on his own account.

In these examples, as previously, the bar-lines are inserted to show the metrical divisions, while the stress marks show where the rhythmical accents are most strongly felt. The rhythmic analysis, it must be repeated, is determined on general principles (already stated), aided by common sense; it is not intended as a dogmatic exposition, in which every detail claims the authority of a papal edict. One or two points claim attention. In Ex. 55 the minim is the unit, and the occurrence of four consecutive 5-note rhythms in the tenor part (commencing at the third beat of the sixth measure) is worth noticing, for the same rhythm prevails at the same time in the alto part, but the accents clash systematically at the interval of a beat. The melodic progression of the tenor in measures 8 and 9 is also unusual in Palestrina, but is explained by the termination of a phrase on the third beat of the ninth measure, the fourth beat being the commencement of a new phrase. In Ex. 56 the signature is C instead of ₵, and the unit is the crotchet instead of the minim. Here one must observe the prevalence of the 3-note rhythm telescoping the 4-note measures, and the ingenuity with which these 3-note rhythms are made to overlap one another in the different parts—a curious complexity which is usually more characteristic of the English madrigalists than the Italian. Another fine instance of the same device is to be found in Josquin des Prés' motet *Ave Maria*, at the section commencing with the words ' Immaculata castitas' (the whole of this motet is quoted in M. Vincent d'Indy's *Cours de Composition musicale*). The next two instances (both from Byrd) call for no particular comment, except that, although the minim is the unit in the first instance and the crotchet in the second, Byrd (with his habitual carelessness in these matters) has used the signature C indifferently in both cases. The careful-ness of Palestrina (as illustrated in the two previous examples) is no less characteristic. In the short extract (Ex. 59, also from Byrd) the feature is the 2-minim sequence in the bass heard against two freely-moving upper parts, in which a 5-minim phrase, treated canonically, becomes prominent. In the last example (a very beautiful one from Wilbye), each part (despite the signature C) starts off in a smoothly-flowing $\frac{3}{2}$ measure, the two lower voices combining to pit their stress against that of the upper one.

In conclusion, a few words about the time-signatures employed in the sixteenth century may not be out of place. The student of musical history will constantly come across the terms Mood, Time, and Prolation, and he should know what they mean. They all refer to the methods of sub-dividing a note into notes of lesser value. Mood expressed the relations of the Long and the Breve : in Mood Perfect, a Long was equal to three Breves, in Mood Imperfect, to two. Time expressed the relation of the Breve to the Semibreve; it likewise could be perfect (sign O or Φ), or imperfect (sign C or usually ₵). Prolation expressed the relation of the Semibreve to the Minim, and could also be perfect ('greater') or imperfect ('lesser'). Its perfection was expressed by means of a dot; in the absence of a dot, Prolation was to be taken as imperfect. By the end of the sixteenth century Mood, in its proper senses, had dis-appeared (though the term was sometimes used loosely as a synonym for Time), and the time-relationships in actual use were the four combinations of Time and Prolation, viz.:

(1) (very rare) Time Perfect and Prolation Perfect (sign O).

$\overset{\circ\cdot}{\rho\rho\rho}\ \overset{\circ\cdot}{\rho\rho\rho}\ \overset{\circ\cdot}{\rho\rho\rho}$ ($\frac{9}{2}$ time in our notation).

(2) Time Perfect and Prolation Imperfect (sign O or Φ).

$\overset{\circ}{\rho\rho}\ \overset{\circ}{\rho\rho}\ \overset{\circ}{\rho\rho}$ ($\frac{3}{1}$ time).

(3) Time Imperfect and Prolation Perfect (sign C).

$\overset{\circ\cdot}{\rho\rho\rho}\ \overset{\circ\cdot}{\rho\rho\rho}$ ($\frac{6}{2}$ time).

(4) Time Imperfect and Prolation Imperfect (sign ₵).

$\overset{\circ}{\rho\rho}\ \overset{\circ}{\rho\rho}$ ($\frac{4}{2}$ time).

Towards the end of the century the sign C was also employed, especially in secular music, to indicate what we should call a $\frac{4}{4}$ measure, the crotchet being the unit, and not the minim. This was quite irrational, for just as O or Φ could be used indifferently for $\frac{3}{1}$ time, so C and Ȼ should, by analogy, have both indicated $\frac{4}{2}$ time. Custom, however, ruled otherwise. This is clearly seen by a perusal of Palestrina's madrigals. In the first book of madrigals (published 1555) the signature is always Ȼ and the time $\frac{4}{2}$; in the second book (published 1586) the signature is always C and the time $\frac{4}{4}$, the treatment of crotchet, quaver, and semiquaver in the latter book corresponding precisely to that of minim, crotchet, and quaver respectively in the former. The English composers were less exact in the matter of notation, as we have already noticed (Exx. 57 and 58). And at the risk of wearying the reader, it must be reiterated that these time-signatures, so far as they indicate a system of accentuation, are purely metrical, such accents being shown only by the conformity of the harmonic procedure in the matter of cadences, suspensions, and so on. To the individual part their significance is entirely non-rhythmical, and merely arithmetical. They show that each measure contains so many semibreves, each of which is in turn equivalent in value to so many minims; they show nothing more than that.

In addition to these time-signatures, the sixteenth century could, by means of the Proportional system, indicate greater complexity in the subdivision of note values. The Proportions were roughly of two kinds: Proportions of Multiplicity, and Proportions of Inequality. The former expressed what we may call geometrical relationships; e. g. by inserting the words Proportio Dupla, or Tripla, or Quadrupla, or simply the signs $\frac{2}{1}$ $\frac{3}{1}$ $\frac{4}{1}$, the composer indicated that each note must now receive only $\frac{1}{2}$, or $\frac{1}{3}$, or $\frac{1}{4}$ of its previous value. Similarly, Proportio sub-dupla, sub-tripla, &c. ($\frac{1}{2}$, $\frac{1}{3}$, and so on), meant that each note had to receive twice, or three times, or four times its previous value. This proportional notation was sometimes useful for supplying the defects of the existing mensural system. The latter, for instance, had no sign to indicate when a minim was to be divided into three crotchets instead of two; but this could be done by the help of Proportion. Suppose a sixteenth-century composer wanted to write a passage sounding as in Ex. 61; Proportion did it for him in the manner shown by Ex. 61 A. The original note-values, of course, could be restored simply by inverting the proportional sign, $\frac{2}{1}$ correcting $\frac{1}{2}$, or vice versa, and similarly with the other proportions. Early in the sixteenth century the Flemish composers habitually employed unnecessary and complex proportions in order to puzzle the layman and guard the mysteries of their craft, but by the end of the century the practice had fallen into disrepute, and the proportions were used mainly, as we saw, for bona fide notational purposes.

The other Proportions—those of inequality—need not trouble us much. Beside the simple geometrical proportions already mentioned, more complex relationships, such as $\frac{3}{2}$, $\frac{4}{3}$, $\frac{5}{4}$, $\frac{7}{4}$, $\frac{8}{5}$, $\frac{10}{8}$, and so on, were recognized in theory. The more elaborate of these were used mainly as a kind of mental gymnastic in the training of singers and composers, and seldom, if ever, found their way into actual composition. The proportion known as *sesquialtera*, however, ($\frac{3}{2}$), was of considerable utility; its effect was to shorten the value of each note by one-third, three of the new notes having to be played in the same time as two of the old. It was the sixteenth-century way of saying ' ♩. = ♩ of preceding '—a direction which is in constant use to-day. There is no reason why the modern student should not try his hand at some exercises in the more unusual combinations; in fact, it is extremely desirable that he should do. But here again he must keep the distinction between rhythmical accent and metrical accent in the forefront of his mind, and not content himself with merely finding, e. g. successive groups of seven notes which may be sung plausibly against successive groups of five notes. To illustrate the difference, Exx. 62 and 63 have been inserted. They are from a hitherto unknown Tudor composer named Bugsworthy. Neither of them is of any great musical value; but it is obvious that while Ex. 62 is purely mechanical, Ex. 63 has demanded some slight mental activity.

The student should perhaps be warned against giving the sixteenth-century notes their nineteenth-century time values. Exact guidance is impossible to give, but one may say that to the sixteenth-century composer a semibreve meant very much what a minim or even a crotchet means to-day. The mind must free itself from the association of 'white notes' with 'slow tempo'. In one example (Ex. 40 A) an approximate transformation of values has been made to emphasize this point; otherwise the note-values in the illustrations are those actually employed by the composer.

IV

MELODY

THE connexion between rhythm and melody is so close that in practice it is dangerous to try and isolate them from each other. Nine times out of ten when we speak of 'melody' we mean 'rhythmic melody'; that is to say, a series of notes whose mutual relationship is considered in terms of accent and duration, and not merely in terms of pitch. All the examples of rhythm quoted in our last chapter were at the same time examples of melody, and once the student has grasped the rhythmic principles followed in the sixteenth century, the remaining details of melodic construction will not cause him the slightest difficulty. The reason why a piece of academic counterpoint never suggests for an instant the melodic outlines of Byrd or Lasso or Palestrina is invariably found to lie in rhythmical misconception. The reader of this volume, it is hoped, will be able to keep clear of such misconception; but a few remarks about the purely melodic elements of the sixteenth-century melody may be of some assistance.

First, as to compass. Every melody must be conceived as being in a definite mode, and as being definitely either in the Authentic or in the Plagal form of that mode. The strict compass of each of these forms has already been given (Ex. 1); it may now be added that in practice a certain extension of compass, upwards and downwards, is usually conceded. The extent of the concession varies slightly amongst the different authorities; but it is substantially defined in these two rules:

(1) That such extension must never exceed a major third in any one direction.

(2) That the total extension (upwards and downwards) must never exceed that of a perfect fourth.

It is recommended, as a matter of discipline, that the student should work within these limits, to which, as a matter of fact, the practice of the Palestrina school conforms very closely. The English composers, however, in this, as in other respects, were a law unto themselves, as may be seen from instances given in Chapter VIII.

Second, as to interval and pitch. Underlying all the rules and observances is the general principle that each part must be easily singable, and if some of the restrictions imposed seem arbitrary, the student must remember that many intervals and progressions which to us (thanks to centuries of harmonic and instrumental training) have become easy and familiar, were by no means easy or familiar to singers who had to find them by the ear alone, with no instrumental doubling to cover up inaccuracies. Unaccompanied singers to-day are sometimes asked to sing progressions that the sixteenth-century singers certainly could not have managed. If they can do so, it is only because such progressions, previously heard on instruments which find the pitch mechanically and without any trouble, have become fixed in their memory, so that their sense of relative pitch is permanently extended.

The general method of melodic construction is expounded by Prof. Wooldridge (*Oxford History*, ii. 376) in the following terms:

'The governing principle, technically speaking, of Palestrina's melody is of course that of conjunct movement; this, however, is beautifully varied by the constantly changing value of the notes [i.e. secondary rhythm] and also by occasional disjunct intervals, *which are permitted upon the condition of not continuing in the direction of the leap, but immediately returning by gradual motion towards the point of departure.*'

The italics are ours; and they are there because the passage is an important one, and undoubtedly gives the clue to one of Palestrina's technical secrets. It is not, however, a rule that can be applied mechanically. Palestrina himself, as Prof. Wooldridge admits, does not so apply it; 'exceptions', he says 'may be found even in his own work', and, as a matter of fact, the exceptions are much more frequent than that 'may be found' might lead one to suppose. The student had better regard it as a maxim for general guidance; that is to say, as a rule which he may infringe, provided that every time he does so he can satisfy himself that he cannot write the passage equally well without infringing it. And in any case, everything depends on the manner of the infraction. The following more specific rules will be found to embody the melodic technique of Palestrina with a fair degree of accuracy:

1. More than two leaps in the same direction are almost always bad; two leaps in the same direction preceded or followed by a step in the same direction hardly less so. Two successive leaps (if taken at all) should be preceded and followed by movement (preferably conjunct) in the opposite direction of the leaps.

2. Subject to this condition, the following pairs of leaps in the same direction are possible occasionally:

(*a*) Perfect fifth ascending or descending, followed by perfect fourth.

(*b*) Perfect fourth ascending or descending, followed by perfect fifth.

(These are fairly common in the bass, but should obviously be used with great caution in any other part.)

(*c*) Major third ascending or descending, followed by minor third.

(*d*) Minor third ascending or descending, followed by major third.

(*e*) Major or minor third ascending, followed by perfect fourth.

(*f*) Perfect fourth descending, followed by major or minor third. (Fourth ascending followed by third, and third descending followed by fourth are less frequent.)

(*g*) Perfect fifth followed by minor third, or vice versa (and still more by a major third), is only permissible in a real emergency.

3. The leap of a minor third is occasionally both preceded and followed by a step in the same direction.

4. Any larger leap, as a rule, is either preceded or followed by movement in the opposite direction. Usually it is the latter: leap followed by step is much more common than step followed by leap.

5. The leaps that can be so treated are those of the major and minor third, perfect fourth, and perfect fifth.

6. Leaps of the octave and of the minor sixth *must* both be preceded and followed by movement in the opposite direction of the leap.

7. The leap of the major sixth is forbidden (exceptions to this rule are rare enough to necessitate its rigid observance).

8. Leaps of an augmented fourth or diminished fifth are forbidden. The common text-book rule permitting the use of the latter in cadence deserves particular denunciation.

9. Not only is the direct leap of these intervals forbidden; care should be taken to avoid any melodic progression that brings them into undue prominence.

10. Leaps of the major and minor seventh are forbidden; also any leap exceeding the octave.

11. The employment of chromatic intervals is forbidden; likewise that of augmented and diminished intervals.

12. The second of two crotchets (if a harmony note) can leap to its octave, or to its fifth (or lesser interval), but not to its minor sixth.

13. Quavers should be employed very sparingly (except in the

cadential formula shown at Ex. 113). They must only be employed in pairs; i.e. as the equivalent of a crotchet; they must be both approached and quitted by step, and they must only be employed *between* the minim beats; never *on* them. The rhythmic figure ♩. ♪ is not used by Palestrina, though it can be found elsewhere.

Rules 12 and 13, as stated, apply in ₵ (i.e. $\frac{4}{2}$) time. In C ($\frac{4}{4}$) time what is here said of crotchets and quavers applies *pari passu* to quavers and semiquavers respectively.

(3) A note can only be tied to a note of equal value, or to one of half its own value; except that at the end of a composition a semi-breve or breve may be prolonged into the final chord. (The student will remember that 'ties' do not, strictly speaking, exist in the music of this period. They are only notes whose value is prolonged beyond the conclusion of the measure; it is convenient to us to use bar lines to show the conclusion of each measure, and therefore ties are sometimes necessary as a matter of notation. If the note is prolonged by half its normal duration, it is perhaps better not to use the tie, but to place a dot on the other side of the bar line.) A tied crotchet (except in C, i.e. $\frac{4}{4}$ time) is of very rare occurrence, and best avoided.

The entire plan of this book is based on the author's conviction that the counterpoint of the sixteenth century should be first approached by way of melody and rhythm, and that the student should make himself thoroughly familiar with the type of melodic-rhythmic outline to be aimed at before attempting the harmonic combination of such outlines in two or more parts. These opening chapters have attempted to set before him the necessary data; specific examples of sixteenth-century melody are not given, because the entire movements quoted in Chapters VI and VII will give him excellent models for a start, and for further specimens he must turn to the scores of the period. By now, probably, he will begin to construct his own melodies, and in addition to what has already been said, the following few points should be borne in mind:

1. The melody should be thought of in long stretches—as long as the duration of one of the movements in a Mass, or of the motets quoted in Chapter VII.
2. It must be written definitely for a particular type of voice, soprano, alto, tenor, or bass as the case may be.
3. It should be set to definite words, Scriptural, liturgical, or secular.
4. Rests should be of sufficient frequency and duration to meet a singer's requirements.

5. Although the melody is for one voice only, yet it must be to
a certain general extent imagined in connexion with other
imaginary voices. The composition as a whole, for instance,
would be punctuated by cadences, and this particular voice
would have to play a definite part in the formation of such
cadences. The student should therefore make up his mind
at what point, and on what degrees of the mode, these
imaginary cadences occur, so that at those points his
melody may shape itself accordingly. It is not necessary
that such cadences should always coincide with the conclusion of a phrase in this particular voice. Sections may
overlap: that is to say, while three out of four voices, perhaps, bring their phrase to its conclusion at a cadence, the
other voice may enter with a new phrase, so constructed as
to assist in the formation of the cadence, but proceeding
on its course without interruption (see, for instance, the
first entry of the tenor in *Veni, Sponsa Christi*, quoted in
full, Ex. 192, or the entry of the alto with the new theme
to the words 'praeparavit in aeternum' in the fiftieth bar of
the same work).

The use of bar-lines is a vexed question which every teacher must
decide for himself. As the incidence of the measure is a real
factor in the construction of the work (see above, p. 17), the present
writer is inclined to recommend regular barring, with a stress mark
($>$) to show the incidence of the rhythmical accents. But if this
is used, it must be clearly understood that it implies nothing in the
nature of a *sforzando*.

V

HARMONY

I. Before discussing the harmonic technique of the sixteenth century in detail, it is well to remind the student that concord is the basis of it all. Discord is an incident, a momentary interruption of concord. Imagine four people walking abreast; one of them stops for an instant, and then has to run to catch the others up; or possibly one of them waits for him, and then the two run together till they have got into line again with the other two. The sixteenth-century view of discord (and it is a mistake to assume without consideration that this view is permanently obsolete) is that of a similar breaking line. Instead of all the parts moving together to the new concord, one of them gets left behind (suspended) for a moment and then the others wait for him to rejoin them, concord being restored as he does so; such interruption is governed by certain clearly defined methods of procedure, which are known as the preparation and resolution of discord; but though some such definition is necessary for the purpose of explanation, it is misleading in so far as it seems to endow the discord with an objective existence. Strictly speaking, the discord itself is merely a method of preparing a fresh concord, and the object of such preparation (not in itself necessary) is to obtain variety of texture, and to enable the different voices to maintain their rhythmic independence. At the same time there is no doubt that the sixteenth-century composers, by constantly employing such procedure, became increasingly sensitive to the emotional effect of discord, and to the possibility of employing it for a harmonic, and not a purely rhythmical purpose.

It is also necessary to be quite clear beforehand as to the number of harmonies that may be employed in a measure or (as it may be convenient to call it) a bar. Many text-books say that two harmonies in a bar are permissible, others, challenging them, that only one can be permitted. Both these views are quite arbitrary and may be disregarded. It all depends on the time-signature. In $\frac{4}{2}$ time ($\mathsf{C}\!\!\!|$) there are four metrical accents in the bar, and thus each minim beat is potentially (not necessarily) a new harmonic unit, i. e. you can have four harmonies in the bar (or three or two or one,

D

but not as a rule more than four).   In $\frac{3}{1}$ time (O or Φ) it depends on the speed of the movement. If the pace is fairly rapid, the semibreve is the unit, and you cannot have more than three harmonies in the measure, intermediate minims being treated as non-accentual. In slower tempo, the minim can be taken as the unit, and a change of harmony is permitted on each minim beat if desired.   In $\frac{6}{2}$ time (C) the measure is divided into two groups of three minims, and each group may have its own three harmonies. Similarly in $\frac{9}{2}$ (O), if the student wants to practise himself in this extremely rare measure, there is no reason why each of the three groups of three minims should not have its own three harmonies. In $\frac{4}{4}$ time (C) the crotchet is the unit, and once more four harmonies are permitted. For the greater part of the period we are considering, the standard duple measure, in sacred music at any rate, was the $\frac{4}{2}$, not the $\frac{4}{4}$, and the student would be well advised to adhere to the former of these, unless he is working to a secular model. And in the latter case he must be quite clear that a bar of $\frac{4}{4}$ is equivalent to a bar of $\frac{4}{2}$, and not to half a bar of $\frac{4}{2}$. The change is purely one of notation.

II. It is assumed that the student has already a knowledge of Elementary Harmony. If he has not, he would be well advised to acquire it from some other source before attempting to master the complicated technique of the period under discussion. With regard to the general method of harmonic progression, all we shall do here is to remind him that (apart from the proper treatment of discord, which will be explained presently) he must depend for his harmonic effect very largely on the variety of sound that can be extracted from the imperfect concord.   This is mainly a matter of spacing and of doubling unexpected notes; any double sounds convincing if it arises naturally from the progression of the parts, i. e. if the note doubled is approached and quitted in both parts by conjunct and contrary motion.   The spacing, too, should always be considered in connexion with vocal colour. If you are writing in five parts, you have five combinations of four different voices available, and by employing the different registers of each voice in varying combinations (e. g. the tenor in his highest register on top, the alto in his lowest at the bottom, and the soprano (low) and bass (high) intermediately, a great variety of colour-effect is obtainable. In six-part writing you have many more four-part combinations available, and, by a similar freedom in combining the different registers, you can get an almost inexhaustible variety of timbre, and your seemingly simple common chords and chords of the sixth become susceptible of constant subtle differentiations of quality. These fine shades are to a sensitive ear more expressive than any gross modern combinations of sounding brass and tinkling cymbal. Never think of your chords in the abstract; think of them not only as chords, but as combinations of vocal colour, and you will soon cease to complain that your material resources are too limited; you will complain, rather, that for their very prodigality you cannot use them to the best advantage. When writing for four voices, let there be frequent passages of two- and three-part writing to vary the fuller four-part combinations, and apply the same principle consistently. In six-part work, for instance, there should be a very moderate amount of six-part writing: the full six-part effect should generally be kept for a climax and for the end of a movement; the six parts being regarded in the main as a reserve, whence an infinite variety of two-, three-, four-, and five-part combinations can be drawn. Even in two-part writing, a judicious contrast of perfect with imperfect concords, combined with a rhythmical conflict, can give the ordinary ear quite enough to engage its undivided attention.

These general remarks, it is hoped, may give the student some ideas as to the best manner of treating the handful of chords—the unison, the perfect fifth, the octave, the major and minor third, the major and minor sixth, and the combinations of these (i. e. $\frac{5}{3}$ and $\frac{6}{3}$ chords), which constitute his harmonic material. There are now certain specific points calling for detailed consideration, viz.:

1. The interval of the fourth and chord of the $\frac{6}{4}$.
2. The use of accented and unaccented passing notes.
3. Changing notes.
4. Suspensions, and the various formulae employed in their resolution.
5. Prohibited consecutives.

These we must examine in their due order.

1. *The Interval of the Fourth.*

The treatment of the fourth is often puzzling to students at first. Scientifically, it is a concordant interval, less concordant than the fifth, but more so than the third or sixth. As harmony developed, and the triad or $\frac{5}{3}$ chord came into constant use, the fourth (which, unlike the fifth and sixth, would not combine with the third) fell into disrepute; moreover, by force of association, it actually acquired the character of a discord. The $\frac{5}{3}$ chord was so frequently preceded by a suspension ($\frac{5}{4}\ \frac{-}{3}$) that the fourth ceased to have the effect of a concord, and was felt to require resolution by the descent of one degree to the third, and ultimately it was only employed in this manner. The interval of the fourth, that is to say, occurring between any of the upper parts and the bass, is a discord, and must be so treated. But between any two of the upper parts it is a concord, and may be sounded freely without preparation so long as it forms part of the harmony of the $\frac{6}{3}$ chord (Ex. 64 illustrates this point; the G's and the C on the second beat of the measure could not be sounded against one another like this if it were not for the E persisting in the bass). Even the augmented fourth is so used, as in Ex. 65, although it is impossible to regard this interval as a concord. But of course both it and its correlative, the diminished fifth, are constantly heard as upper constituents of the $\frac{b6}{b3}$ and $\frac{\sharp6}{\natural3}$ chords, which can be used freely without preparation.

As regards the chord of the $\frac{6}{4}$, it will be clear from the above remarks that it must be treated as a discord. Theoretically, in resolving it, there is nothing to prevent the sixth remaining while the fourth resolves ($\frac{6}{4}\frac{-}{3}$), but in practice the chord is usually treated as a double suspension, resolving on to the $\frac{5}{3}$ chord (see below, Exx. 115 and 122).

2. *Passing Notes.*

Unaccented passing notes of course can be used freely in between two harmonies, the rule being that such notes must be approached and quitted by conjunct motion (the exception to this rule is discussed in the next section, s. v. 'changing notes'). Such notes are commonly of crotchet value, but where the harmony is only changing at the semibreve, the minim *can* also be treated as a passing note (Exx. 66–8). This, however, is somewhat infrequent.

The student should remember that the minim is normally the smallest harmonic unit in $\frac{4}{2}$ measure, and that consequently a crotchet that looks like a new harmony note may have to be treated technically as a discord, i. e. quitted in conjunct movement only. Exx. 69 and 70 illustrate what is meant. In Ex. 69 the second crotchet in the second bar being a constituent of the preceding harmony can be quitted by leap. In Ex. 70 the preceding harmony is the chord of the fifth, and the last crotchet (F), not being a constituent of that chord, must be quitted by step. It cannot be regarded as creating a new harmony of the sixth, and such a progression as that shown in Ex. 71 is not permissible. Exceptions to this rule can be found, but they are very rare.

Double passing notes in thirds and sixths are freely used (Exx. 72 and 73 from Palestrina). The only rule governing such progressions seems to be that once two parts have started on such a series of moving thirds or sixths, the parallel motion is maintained until concord with the remaining part or parts is reached. Such parallel progressions should, however, be used with some restraint; even in Palestrina's hands they often sound perfunctory and conventional.

Often a note in one of the parts (usually the bass) has to do a kind of double duty. Take the progression shown by Ex. 74 (the passage quoted actually occurs in *Assumpta est Maria*, but this and similar progressions are exceedingly common in all the writings of the sixteenth century). It is impossible to explain this chordally in terms that would have been intelligible to Palestrina; but the real explanation is very simple. The B in the bass is a passing note from the point of view of the soprano, but as far as the tenor is concerned it is a harmony note. Similarly the E in the tenor is a discord against the F of the soprano (and its resolution is normal), but tenor and bass are in concord on each beat. The whole passage must be regarded as a complex of three two-part progressions, each of which is in itself perfectly normal and regular, and which may, therefore, be employed in combination. Exx. 75 and 76 afford further illustrations of this in four and five parts. In his own writing, whenever doubtful as to the rightness of a particular progression, the student should apply this test of horizontal analysis, and if the progression stands the test, he can use it without fear. It is obvious that by working on such principles he will obtain (as the sixteenth-century composers obtained) a considerably wider range of harmonic freedom than the text-book rules allow.

Accented passing notes of crotchet value are occasionally taken in any part on the even beats of the measure, in a downward progression, either in $\frac{4}{2}$ or $\frac{3}{1}$ time (Exx. 77–81). If the $\frac{3}{1}$ is fairly fast, minims are constantly treated as unaccented passing notes, but not (so far as the writer's observation goes) as accented passing notes; this applies equally to the $\frac{6}{2}$ (C) time. There seems to have been a tacit agreement that the minim was too imposing a figure to be treated as an accented passing note, whatever the tempo. These accented passing notes should, in any case, be used sparingly, more particularly in the upper part, or their effect is weakened. Orthodox writers like Palestrina avoid using them in an upward progression, and also on the odd beats of the measure. This restriction is in accordance with the accepted metrical rule that the time-signature, though without rhythmical significance as regards the individual parts, does yet indicate a regular system of strong and weak harmonic accentuation throughout the composition as a whole.

3. *Changing Notes.*

The group of instances given in Exx. 82 to 90 will enable us to frame the proper rules for the employment of this formula, which is too cursorily mentioned in existing text-books. It is constantly used for introducing variety of style into composition, but (so far as the most orthodox writers go) always with certain definite restrictions. Subject to these restrictions, the principle is, briefly, that a discordant passing note, instead of falling step by step to the next degree, may fall by the leap of a third to a new harmony note. The governing conditions are :

(a) There is always a group of four notes comprising the formula (Exx. 82–4).

(b) After its leap of a third, the voice concerned must return one degree to the note omitted in its leap.

(c) The first note of the group must be of the value of a dotted minim.

(d) The third note may be of the value of a minim, or of a dotted minim, or of a crotchet, and is, in any case, a harmony note.

(e) If it is a minim, the fourth note will also be of the value of a minim or upwards, and must be a harmony note.

(f) In the other two cases, the fourth note will be a crotchet, and treated as a passing note.

(g) This formula may be employed in any part, and may commence on any beat of the measure ; though Palestrina prefers it to start on one of the even beats.

Apropos of this formula, Parry remarks (*Grove's Dictionary*, s. v. 'Harmony', vol. ii, p. 314) : 'What is particularly noticeable about it is that it gets so thoroughly fixed as a figure in the minds of musicians that ultimately its true significance is sometimes lost sight of, and it actually appears in a form in which the discord of the seventh made by the passing note is shorn of its resolution [i. e. its return one step backward].' As an example he quotes a passage from Byrd's five-part Mass (Ex. 94). This is not historically correct. Earlier writers allow themselves much more freedom in the treatment of the figure, as Ex. 95 will show. This 'irregular' treatment is found repeatedly in writers like Josquin and Pierre de la Rue. The strict method of resolution does not acquire the force of a rule until the latter half of the century, noticeably in the work of Palestrina. Byrd was only following an older tradition, and later still we find John Farmer, in his madrigal 'Take Time while Time doth last' (1599), using the figure exactly as Brumel had used it a hundred years or so before (Exx. 95 and 96). It is worth noticing too that earlier in the same *Credo* Byrd employs the formula strictly *à la* Palestrina. He evidently knew very well what he was about. Appended (Ex. 97) is a curious instance from Palestrina of a double group of changing notes in fourths between alto and tenor, against which the soprano clashes recklessly. The use of the figure in $\frac{3}{1}$ and $\frac{6}{2}$ time is shown in Exx. 91–3.

It will be noticed from Exx. 89 and 90 that the use of the *nota gambiata* (as the Italians call it) can be combined with conjunct movement in one or more of the other parts, even if an incidental clash is thereby created. In Ex. 93 it is seen combined with a suspension in one of the other parts (a not uncommon usage, especially at a cadence).

4. *Suspensions.*

If the note suspended is a concord, of course it may proceed freely, either by conjunct or disjunct motion, and either upwards or downwards. In the case of suspended discords various restrictions have to be observed:

(*a*) Every discord must be preceded by a chord of preparation, and succeeded by a chord of resolution.

(*b*) As a rule, these chords are taken on three successive minim beats, the preparation and resolution occurring on the 'weak' beats of the measure, and the discord itself on the intervening 'strong' beat.

(*c*) But in slow sustained passages semibreve beats may be substituted for minim beats (Exx. 98, 99).

(*d*) More rarely the crotchet beat is substituted for the minim beat (Exx. 100, 101). The student had better avoid this. In the second of these examples, by the way, the first D in the soprano and the first B in the bass are accented passing notes. The second D and the second B are harmony notes, the harmonic skeleton of the passage being shown in Ex. 102. The treatment of the suspension looks at first sight more regular than it actually is.

(*e*) In $\frac{3}{1}$ measure (○ or ⊘) the same principle may be followed, the first, third, and fifth beats being regarded as 'strong', the second, fourth, and sixth as 'weak' (Ex. 103).

(*f*) But more often, if the tempo is fairly fast, $\frac{3}{1}$ time is considered as having three accents only in each measure, discords being prepared on the first beat, taken on the second, and resolved on the third (Exx. 104, 105).

(*g*) In $\frac{6}{2}$ measure (C), each three-minim group is similarly treated, discord being prepared on the first, taken on the second, and resolved on the third minim beat of any group (Ex. 106).

The student may also notice Exx. 107 and 108, in which

the minim is taken as the unit of preparation and resolution
in the first bar, and the semibreve in the second; but
despite Palestrina's authority, there is something to be said
for consistency in treating suspensions, and such instances
are rare.

(*h*) The resolution of a discord is effected by the fall of one
degree in the part suspended (Ex. 109).

(*i*) Such resolution is often given one of the ornamental forms
shown in skeleton form in Exx. 109 to 113. Definite examples from actual composition can be found *passim* in the
illustrations to this and other chapters. The idiom shown
in Ex. 114 is a particularly common formula in cadence.
Ex. 115 is theoretically all right, but not idiomatic.

(*k*) Other ornamental resolutions, such as that shown in Ex. 116,
are very rare, and best avoided, except occasionally to avoid
the consecutives otherwise arising from the resolution of a
suspended fifth, as in Ex. 123. But a number of resolutions
used in the English school will be found in Chap. VIII, and
there is no reason whatever why these should not be employed, provided the student works consistently to an
English model, and does not imagine himself to be writing
in the Roman style.

(*l*) Double suspensions of the third, fourth, fifth, and sixth can be
freely used (Exx. 117 to 126).
    And even that of a complete chord (Ex. 127); cf. also
Ex. 86.

(*m*) A discord and its resolution should not, as a rule, be heard
together in different parts (other than the bass) of the same
chord, except occasionally when the two parts concerned
are both moving in conjunct and contrary motion (Exx. 107,
119, 121). But the resolution is frequently heard in the
bass whilst the upper part is suspended (Exx. 99, 118, 125).

(*n*) While a discord is resolving, one or more of the other parts
may move to a new note of the same harmony (Ex. 128, bar
1), or even create an entirely fresh harmony (Exx. 128
(bar 2), 129).

(*o*) In this way a chain of suspensions can often be formed. The
method of 'horizontal analysis' described above (p. 37) is
usually the only way of explaining such passages theoretically (Ex. 130).

(*p*) A discord may be sounded on the odd beat if the note creating
the discord has been heard as part of the concord on the
previous beat (Exx. 131, 132). Its treatment is then that of

an ordinary suspended discord. This licence is frequent in the madrigalists, but more sparingly used in sacred music.

5. *Prohibited Consecutives.*

The rule prohibiting consecutive fifths and octaves is familiar to every student. He can see for himself that two parts moving in octaves are not independent of one another at all, but merely echoing one another at a higher or lower pitch, and thus not creating a true polyphony. This is true, however, not only of octaves but of any other interval if the sequence continues for any length of time; the consecutive thirds of Brahms, the consecutive major ninths of Debussy, the consecutive minor ninths of Stravinsky, can be quite as mechanical and meaningless as the consecutive octaves, fifths, and fourths of the earliest organum. In any case, the student may well ask, Why are consecutive fifths forbidden absolutely, whereas consecutive thirds and sixths (within reasonable limits) are tolerated ? The present writer can give him no certain answer. The various theories that have been advanced can be disposed of with ludicrous ease ;[1] probably the whole business dates back to Pope John's edict of 1322, which ordained that the perfect concords only should be employed in the music of the Church. The natural perversity of mankind is certain to assert itself against restrictive legislation of this sort, and the inevitable result of the Pope's edict was that the thirds and sixths (under the protective cloak of *faux-bourdon*) became more than ever established in popular favour, while the fourths and fifths fell into a disrepute from which it has been the privilege of the twentieth century to rescue them. To-day it is the turn of the thirds and sixths to be viewed askance by serious composers. However, our present task is not speculative, but practical. We are examining the music of a particular period, and we know (for it can be established inductively) that in that period certain consecutives were as a matter of fact prohibited under certain conditions. The question is merely, What were those conditions ?

Here, once again, the 'rules' of the 'Five Orders of Counterpoint' show that their perpetrators have no intention of consulting the composers whose practice they profess to codify. Let us put them on one side and turn, as usual, to the music ot the period. On the one hand, you do constantly find the progressions shown in Exx. 133–6 ; on the other, you rarely or never find such as those shown in Exx. 137–43—so rarely that when you do find them you may reasonably consider them as an inadvertence. The procedure may be expressed in general form somewhat as follows :

[1] Cf. Dr. Watt's *The Foundations of Music*, chap. xi.

1. Consecutive fifths (and *a fortiori* consecutive octaves) are forbidden between any two parts if no other notes intervene, no matter what the value of the note.
2. Consecutives on successive semibreve beats are broken by the intervention of a minim if it is a harmony note, but not if it is a passing discord. Consecutives on successive minim beats are similarly broken by the intervention of a crotchet if it is a harmony note; not otherwise. (This is the doctrine of Morley, and it is in every way substantiated by sixteenth-century practice.)
3. A suspension may be said to temper the wind to the shorn consecutive. The scholastic rule that 'Passages which would be incorrect without suspensions are equally incorrect with them' is demonstrably out of all relation to the facts.

Consecutive octaves are best avoided even by contrary motion. Consecutive fifths by contrary motion are also best avoided between extreme parts, and in any case when writing for four voices or less. In writing for five or more parts consecutive fifths by contrary motion are not seldom found between two of the inner parts, or even between one outer and one inner part (Ex. 144). The reason is not that such progressions are harder to avoid in five-part than in four-part writing, but that they are less likely to be heard. And consecutives usually forbidden are often tolerated when there is a break in the sense of the words to lessen their 'consequentiality' (Ex. 145). The student should note, too, that such progressions as those shown in Exx. 146 and 147 are continually met with in writers of every school; there is not the slightest objection to the *harmonic* succession of fifths or octaves, provided they do not occur between the same pair of voices.

Some writers lay stress on the avoidance of consecutive major thirds on successive whole degrees of the scale. In two-part writing especially, it is said, the 'tritonal' effect of such a progression is too strongly felt to be endurable. Palestrina, however, seems to have borne it with considerable fortitude (Ex. 148); and in composition for more than two parts passages such as those shown in Exx. 149 and 150 are so common that the rule cannot possibly be maintained.

Consecutive bare fourths are of frequent occurrence between upper parts (Exx. 151, 152); once again one can only remark that the rule forbidding them is out of all relation to sixteenth-century practice. Occasionally you find even a sequence of $\frac{6}{4}$'s (Ex. 153), but this is exceptional and had better not be imitated by the student.

Consecutive unessential discords are occasionally created by the use of accented passing notes; Ex. 154 is an example of a formula to be found in all writers of the period.

Hidden consecutives (fifths and octaves) need not be feared except between the extreme parts. There it is best to avoid them unless one part proceeds by step. Text-books usually specify the step of a semitone, but this restriction is uncalled for. Passages as shown in Exx. 155 and 156 are of common occurrence.

'Chromatic' harmony was not acceptable in sacred music of the sixteenth century. It is obvious that by the help of *Musica Ficta* various augmented and diminished intervals are theoretically possible—E♭ – C♯, for instance, F♮ – G♯, B♮ – E♭, and so on. Such harmony is not, however, in the style of the period, and the ordinary rules of *Musica Ficta* should be disregarded in places where their application would produce one of the chords named, or a similar chord. Secular writers allowed themselves much greater harmonic freedom, so much so that there is no historical sanction for ruling out any progression as impossible. This question will be discussed briefly in Chapter VII, but master and pupil will have to arrange between themselves where the line is to be drawn. As a matter of practical convenience, there is a great deal to be said for observing the same harmonic restrictions whether you are working to a sacred or a secular model. Chromatic harmonies in the music of this period, frequent as they are, have always an air of anachronism; harmonic purity and rhythmical freedom are the most important lessons we have to learn from the sixteenth century.

As various text-books express a pious hope that the student is familiar with what is called 'Modal Harmony', it may be as well to explain in conclusion that such a thing has never existed. 'Modality' is properly a term of melodic definition; it is only in a derivative sense that harmony can be described as 'modal'. In that sense you might say that modal harmony is harmony formed strictly from the diatonic series of notes constituting the mode in which the melody of any given piece is written. In the Dorian mode, for instance, 'modal' harmony would be powerless to sharpen the C or flatten the B. But as we have already seen (Chap. I) this was what the sixteenth-century composers invariably did. As soon as harmony was invented, the modes, through the practice of *Musica Ficta*, tended to lose their modal identity; the Lydian and the Mixolydian became virtually indistinguishable from the Ionian (our major scale), whilst the Dorian was merged in the Aeolian (our melodic minor scale). Any one who speaks of 'modal harmony' as a historic fact can only mean 'the type of harmony that was used by composers of the modal period'. Such harmony is to all intents and purposes our diatonic major and minor harmony in its simplest form, except that tonality in the modern harmonic sense did not yet exist, whilst modulation, as explained above (p. 15), did not mean quite the same thing for Palestrina as it means for us. We shall find presently, however, that the transition from mode to scale is decidedly more advanced in the music of the English composers of this period than in that of their foreign contemporaries.

VI

CANON, FUGUE, AND DOUBLE COUNTERPOINT

FUGUE is apparently a delicate subject; at any rate, it is not usually mentioned in text-books on Counterpoint, and the student is apt to imagine that it sprang suddenly into being, in all its classic symmetry, at the command of J. S. Bach. That is, of course, wrong; Bach invented and brought to perfection many details of fugal construction as we now understand it, but fugue itself is of much greater antiquity. The true descendant of the sixteenth-century fugue is the special type of fugue (so frequently found in the Cantatas of Pachelbel and J. S. Bach) in which some well-known chorale tune is taken, and each of its phrases treated successively as the subject of a fugal exposition; the principle of design here is precisely similar to that of the older fugue written on a *Canto Fermo* taken from Plain-song, of which the motet *Veni Sponsa Christi* (quoted in full, Ex. 192) is an excellent example. The only difference is that the sixteenth-century fugue (as one would expect) is not so straitly bound by the shackles of metre and tonality.

But, in such cases, it is evident that the structural outline is determined very largely by the words themselves, and the student will find many other motets which are essentially similar in general structure, but which are yet not fugal, or (it may be) fugal only in one or two sections. It is better, therefore, to think of fugue not as itself a type of musical pattern or design, but as a method of building up in detail a structure whose main outlines may have been determined on quite other principles. It is, in fact, a procedure, not a form, and the essence of it lies (as we all know) in the imitation by one voice of a phrase or subject previously announced by another.

This was all that was meant by Fugue in the sixteenth century, but of fugue (in this sense) it is possible to distinguish two main types:

1. That in which the imitation is continued strictly throughout— in other words, a canon (whose full description is *fuga per canonem,* 'fugue according to rule').
2. That in which the imitation is discontinued when once the subject has been answered.

Let us postpone the consideration of Canon for the present, and consider the more limited type of Fugue.

1. *Fugue.*

This type corresponds, in the main, to what we understand by the 'exposition' of a fugue. The subject is announced or answered by each voice in turn, and no further allusion need be made to it. The voices proceed in free counterpoint until the composer considers he has dealt sufficiently with this portion of his text and passes to the following section (in which a new theme may be treated in just the same way). At the same time, there is no reason why further reference should not be made to the subject if the composer so desires it, and Ex. 157 (the opening Kyrie of Palestrina's five-part Mass, *Petra Sancta*) well illustrates this more extended type of fugue. The exposition proper, it will be noticed, is complete at the first beat of the ninth measure, whereas the length of the movement is twenty-four measures, and the subject is in evidence almost the whole of the time in one part or another. Considerable use is also made of the subsidiary figure, whose first entry is marked B. There is, however, nothing that could be called a counter-subject, which was the invention of a later period. The modification of the answer at the place marked A is, perhaps, a slight technical flaw, seeing that throughout the rest of the movement the subject invariably appears without modification, but apart from this the workmanship is superb, whilst the grave and austere splendour of the music is such that praise itself seems an impertinence.

This will give the student an idea of what Fugue means (in the sixteenth-century sense); it now remains to discuss one or two aspects of it in detail.

First, as to the subject. This must lie within the strict compass of the mode in which the composition as a whole is written (see above, p. 28); it need not, however, begin on the final of that mode. It may, indeed, begin on almost any note of it. In theory, only certain notes in each mode were permitted (these being known as the Initials or Principals of the mode), but, unfortunately, the theorists could never agree amongst themselves as to which these notes were,[1] and it does not seem necessary to burden the reader with a list of their differences and contradictions. It may be remarked, however, that the first and the fifth notes of the mode are far more often used for commencing than any other, even in the third

---

[1] Cf. the remark of Petrus de Cruce (*Tractatus de Tonis*) : ' Quot differentias seu principia unusquisque eorum [tonorum] habeat, nulla musicae regula numerum certum declaravit.' By ' tones ' he means here ' modes ' ; the two terms were used interchangeably by mediaeval theorists, the so-called ' Gregorian Tones ' being identified with the modes in which they were respectively written—a confusion that is very properly condemned by Glareanus in the *Dodecachordon*.

and fourth modes, although B is not a recognized initial of these modes. The subject may be announced by any voice (subject of course to the practical consideration of compass; a Hypodorian melody, for instance, if not transposed, might not lie well for a soprano, in which case it would be better to announce it in the alto or counter-tenor, and leave the soprano to answer it at the fourth or fifth above).

Next as to the answer. This may take place at the octave or unison, or at the fourth or fifth (above or below). It may be either a strict (or 'real') answer, or a modified answer. The latter often approximates closely to what we should call a 'tonal' answer, fourth constantly being answered by fifth, and vice versa, so that subject and answer between them declare the mode of the composition. There is no rule governing the order of entry of the different voices, nor need the successive entries of subject and answer show any mutual correspondence. Suppose, for instance, the tenor announces a theme in the Dorian mode starting on D, and is answered by the bass starting on A, and that the soprano then enters on D; the alto can now answer him with G if he likes, or with D again if it suits his compass. Between the close of each entry of subject or answer and the beginning of the next entry, 'codettas' (as we should call them) of varying length may be interposed, save only that the first two entries are almost invariably in 'close' order, i.e. the answering voice enters before the statement of the subject is complete, very often at no greater distance than a measure, or even half a measure (Exx. 158 and 159).

For an instance of 'real' fugue, in which the answer corresponds strictly, interval by interval, to the subject, we need look no further than the opening fugue of the motet *Veni Sponsa Christi*, to which reference has already been made in this chapter. Exx. 160 to 167 have been chosen to show the kind of modification to which an answer may be subjected; it will be seen that many of the devices anticipate the 'tonal' methods of J. S. Bach and other composers of a later date. The six-part example from Vittoria is noteworthy; so is that from Tallis, not because of any modification in the answer, but because of the intervals at which the answers are made —a regular system of descending thirds (a precisely similar device appears again later in the course of the same motet). This is quite exceptional.

Skeletons only are given here for the sake of clearness; the sign + means that the harmony is completed by the entry of another voice at the place so marked.

Very often, as a change from the single-part subject, a two-part subject is used, the voices entering, of course, in pairs. Ex. 168 is an instance from Palestrina's Mass *Veni Sponsa Christi* (built, as usual, on the same plain-song melody as the Motet similarly entitled). Here the accompaniment of the melody might almost be called a countersubject, for immediately after the exposition it is used as a melody by the soprano, and then taken up once more by the bass, the whole passage having a charmingly natural and spontaneous air. Ex. 169, from the same composer's *Missa de Feria*, is a similar instance, except that this time the two parts of the subject are treated more deliberately in double counterpoint ; concerning which a few general remarks may not be out of place.

2. *Double Counterpoint.*

First of all, for the benefit of readers who may not have been through a course of Double Counterpoint, a brief explanation seems advisable. Double Counterpoint is sometimes called Invertible Counterpoint, and two themes or subjects are said to be in Double Counterpoint when one of them will serve either as bass to the other's treble, or as treble to the other's bass. (If there are three parts, all of which may similarly change places with each other, they are said to be in Triple Counterpoint, and so on.) There are many kinds of Double Counterpoint, the commonest varieties being those at the octave, tenth, and twelfth (instances of all these will be given in due course). In Double Counterpoint at the octave, one part stands still while the other moves up an octave or down an octave as the case may be. In Double Counterpoint at the tenth, similarly, one part stays while the other moves up or down a tenth. Likewise in Double Counterpoint at the twelfth, one part might stay while the other moved up or down a twelfth ; but in practice, usually, either the bottom part moves up an octave and the top one down a fifth, or the top part moves down an octave, and the bottom one up a fifth. To know whether a given pair of subjects will invert in any of these ways, one must find out what each given interval will become in the inversion, and for this purpose it is only necessary to construct a numerical table and reverse it. In D. C. at the twelfth, for example, the following table is used :

1	2	3	4	5	6	7	8	9	10	11	12
12	11	10	9	8	7	6	5	4	3	2	1

Underneath each interval in the top row is found the corresponding interval with which it will be transformed by this particular form of inversion. Here, for instance, the interval of the sixth becomes that of the seventh, and that is the chief—indeed, the only—difficulty in constructing a piece of counterpoint to invert at the twelfth.

The sixth has to be coaxed and flattered until it consents to turn itself when inverted into a suspended seventh falling one degree at the next step. Other varieties of Double Counterpoint have each their own little difficulties; even at the octave (the simplest form) the harmless fifth inverts into the troublesome fourth, and cannot be used unless it is preceded and followed in a certain manner. All this is to be found in the text-books, but the student will not find the difficulties very formidable, and to overcome them he will do well to rely on experiment and common sense more than on instruction.

Now these three varieties of Double Counterpoint—inversion at the octave, tenth, and twelfth—were familiar to the theorists of the sixteenth century, and practised occasionally by its composers, but not so much, on the whole, as one might expect. In Palestrina one is constantly coming across passages that look as if they were going to be treated in strict double counterpoint, and then somehow they just manage to miss it. Dr. Walford Davies (see his article 'Invertible Counterpoint' in *Grove's Dictionary*) quite rightly scouts the notion that this is due to any lack of theoretical knowledge or of practical competence. No one who studies Palestrina's work can doubt that he had every known device of the period at his finger tips, and that he regarded double counterpoint in just the same light as canonic or proportional ingenuities—that is to say, as a technical discipline, to be quietly mastered and then as quietly discarded, save in so far as it could be made to serve a purely artistic purpose. At any rate, he uses the device very sparingly, and most often in fugue, where he rather likes to announce a subject in two parts and then invert them in the answer. One example of this has already been given (Ex. 169); in Exx. 170 and 171, from the motet *Terra Tremuit*, the inversion takes place at the twelfth. But the composer of this period who really enjoys this harmonic inversion, and employs it systematically, is Luca Marenzio, from whom Exx. 172 to 176 are all taken. He is particularly ingenious at mixing the species; note in Ex. 174 how his counterpoint, by a slight modification in the alto part, is made to finish in the octave after beginning at the tenth, and how in Ex. 175 after starting at the ninth (most intractable of them all) he slithers comfortably into the octave after a few notes. The last of these examples (Ex. 176) is a really fine specimen of triple counterpoint, handled with the utmost assurance and virtuosity.

Besides the harmonic inversion which we call Double Counterpoint, the purely melodic type of inversion can also be found in sixteenth-century music, though this, like its fellow, is evidently

E

a device that was practised assiduously but employed sparingly in actual composition. It too was used frequently (though by no means invariably) to vary the fugal opening. Ex. 177 is the beginning of a madrigal by Sweelinck,[1] in which the subject is answered by strict inversion; the similar treatment of a subject in more than one part is shown in Exx. 178 and 179, both from the indefatigable Marenzio, of whose unfailing dexterity (to tell the truth) one begins to grow rather weary. His sacred music, for all its brilliance, is just a little mechanical, and just a little self-conscious. In Ex. 178 one feels positively grateful to him for not making the inversion strict, as he could easily have done by taking the cantus up to C at the second beat of the fourth measure.

3. *Canon.*

Canon has already been defined as a special type of fugue in which the imitation is not discontinued after the subject has been answered, but carried on continuously through the whole of a movement, or at any rate, for some considerable period, each phrase as it is given out by the *vox antecedens* being taken up and answered by the *vox consequens*. Such imitation may take place at any interval, simple or compound, either above or below. In a composition for more than two voices, it is not necessary that all should take part in the canon; very often, for instance (as in Ex. 183) two voices only are treated in canon, the other parts moving in free counterpoint; such a canon is spoken of as a canon 'two in one', at the unison (or fifth below, or tenth above, or whatever the interval may be). If the *vox consequens* is in turn imitated by a third voice, the canon is spoken of as a canon 'three in one', and so on. Or you may leave two or more canons worked simultaneously in the same composition by four or more voices; in this case the canon is known technically as a canon 'four in two'. Byrd's *Diliges Dominum* (part of which is quoted in Ex. 185) is actually, as will be seen, a canon 'eight in four', with the additional ingenuity that in each pair of voices the part of the lower is that of the upper begun at the end and sung backwards, i. e. a canon *per recte et retro*.

It will be noticed that even Byrd cannot make the parts particularly interesting, and has to allow himself a good deal of freedom. The first two notes of the second tenor, for instance, make octaves by contrary motion with those of the second bass, whilst the second and third notes of the second tenor also make octaves by contrary

---

[1] From Mr. Barclay Squire's *Ausgewählte Madrigäle.*

motion with those of the first bass.   The canon is nevertheless an astonishing *tour de force*.

A Canon is not only stricter than a Fugue by virtue of its length; it is stricter in form also.   This is illustrated by a passage in Morley's *Plaine and Easie Introduction* (1597), where the pupil, observing that, in a specimen fugue given him for perusal, the interval of a fourth is answered by that of the fifth, asks if this is not irregular.   'No', replies the master, 'although it rise five notes, yet is it the point (i. e. the subject).   For if it were in canon, we might not rise one note higher nor descend one note lower than the Plainsong did; but in Fugues we are not so straitly bound.'

That is to say, in Canon, the intervals of the answer must correspond to those of the subject, third answering to third, fourth to fourth, fifth to fifth, and so on.   At the same time, it is not necessary that the intervals should be identical (unless the canon is at the unison or octave, when each phrase of the *vox consequens* is usually an exact repetition of that previously announced by the *vox antecedens*).   Elsewhere, a major second may often be answered by a minor, and vice versa, and so with the remaining intervals.   This is shown clearly by two or three illustrations (Exx. 180-2) taken from Palestrina's *Missa ad Fugam,* which may be considered the *locus classicus* for the study of the sixteenth-century canon.   It is not musically one of his most valuable works; he wrote it doubtless to satisfy himself that he had a perfect command of canonic device, just as he wrote his mass on *L'Homme Armé* (like Josquin and so many of his contemporaries), to show that he was thoroughly at home in the labyrinth of Proportional Combination.   The *Missa ad Fugam* should be regarded mainly as a masterpiece of technique, and from that point of view it is certainly deserving of study.   We also give two more extended examples of Canon, both from Palestrina. The first (Ex. 183) is part of the last movement of the *Missa Brevis,* the canon being in this case a canon 'two in one at the unison' carried on between the two upper voices.   The subject of the canon is, at the same time, it will be noticed, the subject of a five-part fugue; but whereas the three lower voices are set free after they have answered the subject, the two upper ones maintain their strict canon at the unison right up to the end of the mass. The other example (Ex. 184) is slighter in form, and rather more ingenious—a three-part movement which takes the form of a canon 'three in one', for men's voices only.   None of the parts therefore is free, whilst the interval at which the answer is made—that of the second above—calls for more dexterous management than an answer at the unison.   Even Palestrina's resources are taxed in one or two places, notably in measures 9 and 10, 24 and 26, for which Palestrina would probably have been ploughed in a Mus. Bac. examination; but if the method of 'two-part horizontal analysis' is applied (as explained on p. 37) it will be found that the harmony is in each case perfectly correct. The whole piece, moreover, is delightful as music, especially the final cadence, which is at once entirely unexpected and entirely convincing.

From the practical point of view that is, perhaps, as much as the student need know about the use of canon in sixteenth-century composition. It was a recognized branch of the art, but was not employed with any great frequency. In this we may see a reaction against the canonic debauches (one can use no other word) of the preceding period. Ockenheim, Josquin des Prés, Pierre de la Rue, and other composers of the late fifteenth and early sixteenth century delighted in displaying a most perverse ingenuity in the construction of canons. Canons by augmentation, Canons by diminution, Canons *per recte et retro*, Canons *cancrizans*, puzzle Canons of every description, were poured out in their hundreds by these too ingenious minds, and they were usually inserted in the one place where they were peculiarly inappropriate—the setting of the mass. To make them as difficult as possible for the singers, one voice only was written out, on a single stave, the other voices being expected to take their cue from some enigmatical Latin motto prefixed; thus a Canon *per recte et retro* would be indicated by the words 'Canit more Hebraeorum', 'Iustitia et Pax se osculatae sunt', and so on; 'clama, ne cesses', 'Otia securis insidiosa nocent' meant that the answering voice was to take no notice of rests, but to pass straight from one note to the next; canons by augmentation or diminution were often indicated simply by a bewildering multiplicity of time-signatures placed at the beginning of the single stave, and so on. Padre Martini enumerates (in Part II of the *Saggia di Contrappunto*) no less than fifty-six of such enigmas, taken from compositions of this period. Canon was in fact a new toy, and it was natural that musicians should spend most of their time playing with it, and seeing how many new games they could invent. It all helped in the development of musical technique, and did no harm beyond wasting a good deal of the singer's time, and creating a certain flutter in the ecclesiastical dove-cotes. The return to sense and sanity came in due course, and it was Palestrina who led the way.

VII

DESIGN

THE purpose of this chapter is to explain briefly the main types of choral design followed in the sixteenth century; that is to say, in sacred music, the Mass and the Motet; in secular music, the Madrigal. The instrumental forms lie outside the scope of this volume; at the same time, one may remind the reader that interesting experiments were being made, and that in the Fitzwilliam Virginal Book, in *Parthenia*, and similar collections he will find the first attempts in many directions which later composers were only too glad to follow up, the suite, for instance, the Air and Variations, the Fantasia, and the Toccata. Similar exploration, of course, was being carried out in other countries besides England, but the volumes just mentioned are those most easily accessible to an English student.

1. *The Motet.*

The Motet is an ancient form of music, and the very derivation of its name is uncertain. Modern theory is inclined to associate it with the French *mot* and to explain *motetus* (whence 'motet') as a later Latinized form. That may well be so; in any case, by the sixteenth century the word was understood (and had long been understood) to mean a piece of unaccompanied vocal music, of moderate length, and of a sacred character, the words being taken, as a rule, from scripture or from the liturgical books. The general principle of design in every case is the same; the text is analysed, and each clause of it treated musically as a more or less complete section, ending, as a rule, with a clearly defined cadence on one of the regular modulations of the mode (see p. 15), the cadence of the last section being, of course, on the final (the reader will understand from Chap. II why it is better to speak of the 'final' rather than the 'tonic'). For each section the composer had, roughly, three methods of treatment at his disposal: (1) the fugal, (2) the chordal, (3) the intermediate, in which the texture is clearly polyphonic and not harmonic or chordal, and yet not fugal. There is no reason why the three methods should not be combined in a single motet, one section being in free polyphony, the next in chords, the next a set fugal exposition, and so on; but for the sake of clearness the motets

chosen to illustrate this chapter are compositions in which a single
method is pursued consistently from start to finish.

The first, Palestrina's four-part motet, *Veni Sponsa Christi*, is
an example of the fugal method. Words and melody form an antiphon, which may be found, of course, in its proper liturgical place.
The melody is treated strictly as a *Canto Fermo* (not in the scholastic
sense!), and it is therefore reproduced at the head of the composition,
so that the student may more easily follow the method of musical
construction. The notation in semibreves is conventional; the
rhythm of plain-song follows the natural stress of the spoken word,
and therefore cannot be exactly reproduced in modern musical
notation.

Now let us turn for a moment to the text. This runs as follows:

> Veni, Sponsa Christi, accipe coronam, quam
> tibi Dominus praeparavit in aeternum,

which may be translated thus:

> Come, thou Bride of Christ, receive the diadem
> which the Lord hath prepared for thee for ever.

The whole motet consists of sixty-seven measures, divided here as
usual (for the sake of convenience) by bar-lines, and apportioned to
the text as follows:

> Measures 1–19.   Veni, Sponsa Christi.
> „   20–39.   Accipe coronam.
> „   39–50.   Quam tibi Dominus.
> „   51–67.   Praeparavit in aeternum.

Each of these sections is a complete fugue (in the sixteenth-
century sense, explained in the last chapter), and the subject of each
is based strictly on the section of melody to which the corresponding words are sung in the antiphon, the four themes being shown
in Exx. 188–91. Before going any further, one must point out how
very wide of the mark is the prevailing impression that sixteenth-
century counterpoint is 'formless' or 'vague in structure'. We
have already seen that this same counterpoint, so often declared to
be 'rhythmless', is above all things the art of combining rhythms,
whose 'irregularity' is most skilfully regulated; now we see that
its design, so far from being inchoate or muddled, is extremely
severe, and highly organized. There is no uncertainty in the
thematic definition; the modulation is firmly controlled; the
whole thing is clear in conception and logical in execution.

A few points are worth mentioning. The mode is G. Tenor and
cantus are in the authentic compass, alto and bass in the Plagal, the
concessions in each case being well within the limits mentioned at

the beginning of Chap. IV. The composition as a whole, therefore, is (by convention) in the seventh mode (not transposed). Its length is sixty-seven measures, but only thirty-six of these are in four-part harmony, the remainder being in three parts or less. In the opening fugue, the first part of exposition is given to cantus and alto in close order, the remainder of it being an exact repetition at the octave by tenor and bass. In each of the other fugues (commencing respectively at measures 20, 39, and 51), the order of entry is different, but each time the answer is a real answer. The second fugue is irregular in two ways; first, the theme is never announced by itself, each entry being accompanied by free counterpoint in two or more of the other parts (doubtless for the sake of variety); second, the theme appears twice in the tenor (measures 20 and 26) before it is heard at all in the bass, whose first thematic entry is at measure 28. The modulations which conclude each main section, viz. G (measure 19), C (measure 38), D (measure 50), and of course, the final close on G, are all perfectly regular. The motet, also, though selected chiefly as a specimen of fugal construction, illustrates several points of composition mentioned in earlier chapters of this volume:

(1) Measure 14. The leap to the octave from the second of two crotchets is worth noticing.

(2) Measures 26 and 28. The harmony is justified by 'two-part horizontal analysis'.

(3) Measures 28–30 (tenor part). Note the charming way in which the three quadruple measures are telescoped by four $\frac{3}{2}$ rhythms. Another telescope may be seen in the last of these measures, where the C does double duty as the last of one group of changing notes and the first of another, the rhythm of the whole passage being delightfully subtle and intricate.

(4) In measures 36–8 (bass part) the double skip of fourth followed by fifth is preceded by a step from outside; but thanks to the long pause on the C in measure 36, and the clearly cadential nature of the passage, the melodic irregularity is more perceptible to the eye than to the ear.

(5) In the last section, note the persistency with which the theme (tenor) insists on being heard up to the very end, and the way in which the C, softening into B, prepares the ear for the final cadence, whose F♯ sounds particularly refreshing after the obstinate F♮ sustained by the bass in the previous measure—a progression impossible in the tonal system of the eighteenth and nineteenth centuries, but one whose rare beauty we can begin to appreciate in the twentieth.

Our next example, from the six-part motet, *Tu es Petrus* (also by Palestrina), is constructed by quite a different method. The motet is rather too long to be quoted entire in this book, but the section quoted (Ex. 193) is of sufficient extent to illustrate the method employed, and the same method is pursued consistently throughout the composition, in which there is no trace of fugue, and at the same time hardly any plain chords or note-against-note counterpoint, except in one passage where for half-a-dozen measures or so, at the words 'non praevalebunt', the voices divide into two three-part choirs, answering each other antiphonally with chords.

The text is as follows :

'Tu es Petrus, et super hanc petram | aedificabo Ecclesiam meam | et portae inferi | non praevalebunt adversus eam : | et tibi dabo claves regni coelorum ("Thou art Peter, and on this rock I will build my church, and the gates of hell shall not prevail against it; and I will give thee the Keys of the Kingdom of Heaven ").'

These words are sung in Church to a melody that is virtually the same as *Veni Sponsa Christi*, already quoted ; the motet *Tu es Petrus*, however, is not built on a *Canto Fermo*, and its themes are not taken from the plain-song melody at all. Nevertheless, the general principle of design is to this extent the same, that each section of the text forms the basis of a clearly marked musical section. The mode is again G (authentic) and the principal closes (apart from those on the Final) are all on C (measures 20, 24, 32, 47, and 51). The closes are unusually frequent and emphatic, and the whole composition gives the impression of a firmness and solidity as clear-cut and stable as the very rock itself. The length of the work is 84 measures, of which, roughly,

22 measures are in three-part harmony
34   „   „   four-part   „
10   „   „   five-part   „
18   „   „   six-part   „

This table gives us the clue to the musical design, which is built up by contrasting different groups of voices with one another, every possible variety of timbre being employed, and the forces gradually increased, until everything is ready for a climax, when they all join to produce a massive six-part harmony. Thus, in the opening section (which is quoted) the two cantus parts and the alto start off and deliver a sharply-defined musical phrase of six measures' length, in three-part harmony. This is answered verbatim, an octave lower, by tenor, sextus (whose compass is here roughly that of a baritone), and bass. Then, for the next twelve measures, the three-part harmony is enlarged to four parts, the following combinations being successively employed: 13–15, C, C 2, A, S; 16–19, C, A, T, B; 20–24, C 2, A, T, S. Then, for the first time, the full six-part harmony is employed, and continues until the thirty-second measure, when the first main division of the motet ends with a full close on C. The rest of the work is built on precisely similar lines. The method is essentially architectural, and the effect cumulative. The writing itself is perfectly straightforward, the only point that calls for comment being the bold use of the chord E C G in measure 23, where it is treated as a passing chord and for the space of a minim beat is heard clashing against the sustained F of the cantus part above.

As an example of the shorter and simpler type of motet is subjoined (Ex. 194) Palestrina's *O Bone Jesu*. Here the texture is, in the main, chordal (the second of the three classes mentioned above, *Tu es Petrus* being an example of the third), and there are no complications. At the same time the progression of each part is always interesting; there is just enough movement every now and again to cast a ripple, as it were, over the surface, just enough discord to vitalize the music, without disturbing its essential simplicity. There is no elaboration of the text, almost every syllable of which receives its own note of melody. A large number of sixteenth-century motets are of this short and simple character, and very often they are of extreme beauty; more touching, perhaps, and more immediate in their appeal than their larger and more intricately wrought fellows. Technically, perhaps, we cannot learn much from them, for their purpose is purely devotional, and they make no pretence to elaboration of workmanship. But by the contemplation of a flawless work of art, however small, however simple, every one is in some measure enriched, and that must be the justification for inserting this motet in a book which professes to be purely technical in purpose. Even in these few chords, it will be noticed that Palestrina contrives to violate several of the text-book maxims; in measure two, for instance, the unison is approached by similar motion, in measure seven by oblique motion; in measures eight and nine in the cantus and alto parts, the consecutive perfect fifths B–E and A–D are simply 'dodged' by a suspension: in measure twenty-three the cantus and alto proceed in consecutive major thirds descending one whole degree, the two lower parts holding the D as though to ensure the forbidden tritone in the upper parts being given full prominence. It needs no great insight to see how easily each of these irregularities could have been avoided by a composer who attached any great importance to them, the inference being, inevitably, that Palestrina did not.

2. *The Mass.*

The words of the Mass need not be quoted here. The essential thing to be remembered by the student of musical design is that they fall into six main divisions:

(1) The Kyrie.   (2) The Gloria.   (3) The Credo.
(4) The Sanctus.   (5) The Benedictus.   (6) The Agnus Dei.

Of these, the Gloria, Credo, and Sanctus are sections of considerable length, resolving naturally into smaller groups or sub-sections. In a colossal work like Bach's B minor Mass, each of these sub-sections is treated as a separate movement; but in the masses of the sixteenth century, intended for strict liturgical use, it was not feasible to work on such a scale, and the Mass was designed, as a rule, to give some sense of textual continuity. Subject to this restriction, however, the dimensions of the Mass vary a good deal; thus Palestrina's mass, *O Admirabile Commercium*, is some 650 measures in length, whereas the same composer's *Iste Confessor* is but 370. The difference arises from precisely the same cause as the corresponding variety in the length of the Motet. Of the two motets quoted in full in this chapter, *Veni Sponsa Christi* and *O Bone Jesu* (Exx. 192 and 194), the former is 67 measures long, the latter only 24, whereas the text in each case is of roughly the same length, and in each case resolves into four sections. The difference in the length of the composition is due entirely to the method of musical treatment, the fugal method involving as a rule a good deal of textual repetition, whereas in plain note-against-note counterpoint the text can be set continuously, with no repetition at all if the composer so desires.

In the Mass as in the Motet, examples of each kind can be found: Palestrina's *Missa ad Fugam*, as already remarked, is strictly fugal throughout, the *Missa Assumpta est Maria* is polyphonic in texture but not consistently fugal, while Orlando Lasso's *Missa Quinti Toni* is predominantly chordal. But more often the method is mixed, certain sections (especially the Kyrie, Benedictus, and Agnus Dei) being treated fugally, while the more exegetical parts of the text— e. g. the Credo—are set more simply.

In the Mass, of course, one mode as a rule prevails (except in masses for a special occasion, such as the Mass for the Dead, which differs both in text and construction from the ordinary mass), and very often the title of the Mass is taken from the mode in which it is written— e.g. *Missa Quarti, Quinti, Sexti,* &c., *Toni,* and even *Missa cuiusvis Toni.*[1]

---

[1] Or 'Mass in any mode you like', an ingenious composition by Ockenheim or Ockeghem, a famous composer of the fifteenth century. In this mass the mode can be

But more often the Mass takes its title from the *Canto Fermo* on which it is built; this is very often a plain-song melody (e. g. the mass *Veni Sponsa Christi*) or a Latin hymn (e. g. *Aeterna Christi Munera*), but the composer might write on his own themes if he likes, or on a folk-song (cf. the numerous masses on *L'Homme Armé*, or those by Tye and Taverner on *Westron Wynde*). Some of Palestrina's masses (e. g. *Vestiva i Colle* and *Nasce la gioja mia*) are based on themes taken from madrigals by himself or other contemporary writers. The theme is usually treated with great rhythmic freedom; in Exx. 195–195 D will be found some of the guises in which the opening strain of *Aeterna Christi Munera* is presented in Palestrina's mass of that name, and Taverner's *Westron Wynde* is another example that will repay study. The sixteenth-century Mass on a *Canto Fermo* has, indeed, a close affinity with the modern theme and variations, and also with such 'cyclic' symphonies as Liszt's 'Faust' Symphony and Berlioz's *Symphonie Fantastique*, in which a single thematic germ reappears in various transformations throughout all the movements of the work. But the most interesting modern adaptation of sixteenth-century structural principles is to be found in Vincent d'Indy's string quartet in E (op. 45). Every student of Counterpoint may be recommended to make a thematic analysis of that work (which is published in miniature score), for nothing will show him more convincingly how much a modern composer may learn from the methods of Palestrina.

3. *The Madrigal.*

Some account of the Madrigal will naturally be looked for in this chapter, but the Madrigal was never for music, as for literature, a formal type of structure. The name connotes a spirit rather than a form; it is not possible to lay down in theory any hard and fast rules for its composition, and in practice it is equally impossible to trace any clear dividing line between the Madrigal so-called, on the one hand, and such kindred varieties of secular music as the Chanson, the Canzonet, and the Ballet on the other. All one can say is that the term Madrigal is of wide and vague application, but that on the whole it is the secular equivalent of the Motet, in so much as its general outline and character depend on the words chosen for setting, whilst the musical texture employed is commonly

altered at will by changing the position of the clefs on the stave. For a detailed explanation see Ambros, *Geschichte*, iii. 178, also Michel Brenet, *Musique et Musiciens de la vieille France*, p. 65. Quotations from this mass can be seen in the *Oxford History of Music*, vol. ii, p. 213, but Professor Wooldridge has missed the real clue to the title, which is the adjustment of the clef.

a mixture of the chordal, the polyphonic, and the fugal, these words being used in the same sense in which they have already been taken to define the three outstanding types of motet. The technical difference between the Madrigal and the Motet, in fact, is one of style rather than of form, and the purpose of the concluding section of this chapter, despite its title, is not to investigate formal differences, but to emphasize some of the differences in style which distinguish the secular music of the sixteenth century from the sacred music of the same period. If for the sake of brevity and convenience the term Madrigal is employed, as it frequently will be, the student will understand that the characteristic features we shall discover are to be found equally in secular compositions bearing other names. For the moment, in short, the term will be used generically to represent its class, just as the term Motet, so far as technical style is concerned, will be taken as representing various other types of sacred music, such as Hymns, Graduals, Lamentations, Improperia, and so on.

First of all as to Mode. From the early part of the century composers had allowed themselves much greater latitude in the use of *Musica Ficta* when writing madrigals than when writing for the church. The accidentals permitted by *Musica Ficta* were introduced not merely to form a cadence or to avoid the tritone, but to create chromatic progressions in the melody; whilst the accidentals not so recognized (D♯, A♭, and so on) were gradually and tentatively introduced [1] one by one, until by the end of the century a complete scheme of chromatic harmony and modulation was within the grasp of a really adventurous musician. The tendency in its extreme form may be seen in the works of Carlo Gesualdo, Prince of Venosa, from whom Exx. 196 to 198 are taken. Such passages in no sense represent their age; in fact they are clearly symptomatic of a decline, in their reliance on the easy blandishments of harmony, and their neglect of the more vital elements, rhythmical continuity and firmness of outline. The voices in these madrigals were no doubt doubled by instruments—a custom that had been growing in frequency. The necessity of this will be apparent to any one who tries to sing Ex. 198 without the assistance of a piano. The student must not for an instant think that these are typical specimens of madrigalian writing. They are, nevertheless, a logical though extreme development of what had been going on for a long time, notably in the work of Orlando Lasso, who shows, even in his sacred

---

[1] For an exhaustive (not to say exhausting) account of chromatic experiment in the sixteenth century, see Kroyer, *Die Anfänge der Chromatik im italienischen Madrigal des XVI. Jahrh.*

music—in the Penitential Psalms, for example—a strong liking for realistic illustration, and whose madrigals naturally exhibit the same tendency. Exx. 199 to 201 show the way in which he endeavoured to employ chromatics to illustrate such phrases as 'lagrime nove' (Ex. 199), 'mutato stile' (Ex. 200), 'dolcezz' amare' (Ex. 201; the C♯ here is vouched for by Sandberger, editor-in-chief of Breitkopf and Härtel's complete issue of Lasso's work). Precisely the same chord (augmented sixth) is used by Wilbye in his madrigal 'My Throat is sore' (First set, No. 27) to illustrate the words 'my song runs all on sharps'. He probably knew Lasso's work, but is more likely to have learnt the chord from Byrd, who, with characteristic audacity, uses it in a motet (*Civitas Sancti tui*).[1] Other well-known instances of chromatic progression on a considerable scale are to be found in the madrigals of Cipriano di Rore, and among the Englishmen, of Weelkes, who uses the device both melodically (as at the end of 'Cease Sorrows now') and harmonically (as at the beginning of 'Hence Care, Thou art too cruel'). Occasional chromatics are indeed too common in the madrigalian writing of the sixteenth century to need illustration, or at any rate further illustration than is afforded by the examples already quoted. But a particularly happy employment of the device by Wilbye to illustrate a parenthesis is quoted from his madrigal 'Thou art but young, thou say'st' (Ex. 202). One of the strongest features of the English madrigalists is their ability to introduce such occasional touches of realism into their work without allowing the habit to master them; in the Italian madrigalists the structural continuity and melodic outline are often sacrificed fruitlessly in the attempt to illustrate every tiny detail of the words.

In a brief and summary account like the present it is difficult to describe and illustrate the harmonic licenses to be found in the madrigalian writers without appearing to assign an undue importance to such things, but as a matter of fact you can turn page after page without finding anything to dismay the orthodox. The best madrigalists of the best period rely more on rhythm and general lightness of treatment than on recondite harmonies and unexpected chromatics. The gist of the matter is well expressed by Morley in his *Plaine and Easie Introduction*:

'In no composition shall you prove admirable except you put on and possess yourself wholly with that vaine wherein you compose, so that you must in your musicke be wavering like the wind;

---

[1] The MSS., however, are not unanimous. See Walker, *History of Music in England*, p. 345. On *a priori* grounds the D♯ is improbable; Byrd uses strange flats more freely than strange sharps.

sometimes grave and staide, otherwhile effeminat; you may main-
taine points and revert them, use triplaes [i. e. triple proportion]
and show the verie utmost of your varietie, and the more varietie
you show, the better you shall please . . . we must also take heed
of separating any part of a word from another by a rest, as some
dunces have not scrupled to do . . . you may set a crotchet or
minim rest above a comma or colon in the dittie, but a larger rest
than that of a minim you may not make till the sentence be
perfect. . . . Lastly, you must not make a close (especially a full
close) till the sence of the words be perfect.'

Morley carried out his own precepts with consummate skill; in
mastery of rhythmic device he is second to none of his own or of
any other period. Some examples from his pen might well have
been inserted here, but, on the whole, they seem more appropriate to
the next chapter, in which an attempt is made to define some of
the peculiarities which distinguish the English music of the sixteenth century from that of other schools. The example chosen to
illustrate the madrigal style (Ex. 203) is nevertheless from the
English school—the six-part ' Draw on, Sweet Night ', from John
Wilbye's second set of madrigals. It is too long to quote entire,
but its artistic beauty alone would justify its choice. There is no
far-fetched attempt at pictorial illustration in it, yet the opening
pages bring to our minds an almost physical sense of twilight and
deepening shadow; and has any composer ever voiced more beautifully than Wilbye, at the thirty-second measure, the contrast
between the serene mystery of nightfall and the anguish of the
lonely human whom the night encompasses?
The harmony is curiously modern, not in the employment of
chromatic intervals, but rather in the avoidance of them, and the
preference for bold and simple effects—the sustaining of the
double A, for instance, in the sixteenth measure, and the powerful
suspensions in the twenty-seventh, twenty-eighth, and twenty-ninth
measures, which are worthy of J. S. Bach himself, and indeed
anticipate in a singular manner such passages as the opening of the
middle section of the Organ Fantasia in G major. The chord of
the dominant seventh in the twenty-eighth measure need not startle
us, for Byrd, as we shall see, had been using it in very similar
fashion for twenty years or more. Of course the piece is entirely
non-modal; despite the flat in the signature, the opening section
of the madrigal is plainly in the diatonic key of D major, with
touches of dominant and sub-dominant in the nineteenth and
twenty-first measures respectively. At the entry of the words ' My
life so ill ' there is an abrupt change to the tonic minor, followed
three bars later by a perfectly orthodox modulation to its relative

major. The principle throughout is that of key, not of mode, and the same may be said of nearly all the English madrigals. It should not be thought, however, that this tendency is universal; it naturally becomes more marked towards the end of the century, and in the work of Gesualdo, as we have seen, almost every trace of modal writing has been obliterated. But the earlier madrigalists— Arcadelt, Willaert, and their immediate successors—kept pretty closely to the dictates of the modal system, and so to a large extent does Palestrina; in his first set of madrigals, for instance, the first six numbers are all written strictly in the Phrygian or Hypo-phrygian mode transposed—in A, that is to say, with a B♭ in the signature.

In conclusion, it may be said, perhaps, that although the fugal principle runs all through the Madrigal, and although numerous madrigals can be found in which the answer is strict and the exposition regular, yet the tendency is to greater freedom than composers usually allow themselves in the Motet. The formal Fugue is replaced by a fugue of imitation, in which the answer makes little pretence of corresponding, interval by interval, with the subject, but is content to reproduce its rhythmic shape. The subject, too, is often shorter, a mere 'point', it may be, of some three or four notes, which is quickly taken up by the other voices, and then as quickly abandoned. Naturally, the style depends largely on the sentiment of the words, for the Madrigal is not necessarily light-hearted. But greater freedom is not incompatible with proper dignity, and the formalities of double counterpoint and strict canon are out of place, generally speaking, even in madrigals of the more serious type.

VIII

SOME TECHNICAL FEATURES OF THE ENGLISH SCHOOL

No apology is needed for devoting part of a book that is intended primarily for English students to a consideration of the specially English methods of composition, which differed in many important respects from those of contemporary foreign composers. It is only with the technical aspect of these differences that we are now concerned; it may be remarked, however, that every technical difference, whether between one man or another, or between one school and another, probably has a psychological counterpart, and really implies a corresponding difference in outlook. In the music of Schumann and Purcell, for instance, we are conscious of a profound emotional and spiritual difference, but that difference can only be expressed in music by technical means; if Schumann wants to express in music a certain set of convictions or states of mind, his music is bound to reveal a predilection for certain types of harmony, of rhythm, of texture, for these are the elements of musical speech. This fact is too often forgotten by those who decry all technical criticism, or at best concede it a purely technical interest. They may themselves not be able to follow such criticism, they may be unable to deduce the spiritual from the technical, and it would be unreasonable to demand that they should be able to do so. But this incapacity, though it is not their fault, is certainly their misfortune, for in the technique is the clue to the personality. There is, of course, an incapacity precisely opposite; a man may have made himself mechanically familiar with musical technique, and yet have no true musical understanding. He is in far worse case, for the composer's message never reaches him at all, whereas the others, though liable to misconception, can grasp its essential purport. The real musician, who is bound by neither of these limitations, can well afford to spend some time on considerations of a purely technical character. He will not mistake the means for the effect, but he will realize that you cannot have the one without the other; in the idiosyncrasies of the craftsman he will try to discern the mentality of the artist. And in the peculiarities of English sixteenth-century craftsmanship, viewed as a whole, he will find much that is significant, much that will widen his understanding of his own musical ancestry. And the composer of to-day who can retranslate what he has thus learnt in terms of modern musical technique is the man who is going to help to restore the true English musical tradition.

First of all, then, as to Mode. The sixteenth-century Modal System, as we saw, was a compromise, in which all the modes tended to lose their identity, and to merge into two general types, clearly foreshadowing our own major and minor scales. The English composers at a comparatively early date seem to have felt that the compromise was doomed, and that a two-scale system must replace the old ecclesiastical modes (of which Morley speaks, in the *Plaine and Easie Introduction* of 1597, as something quite antiquated and remote). Even the Phrygian mode, which retained a good deal of its individuality, was roughly handled by the Englishmen. In Tallis's *Lamentations*, for instance (composed probably about 1580), the prevailing mode is Phrygian, but in the middle, at the words 'plorans ploravit' ('she weepeth sore in the night'), comes a section whose tonality can only be described as the diatonic key of B♭ major—a collocation unheard of at that time, and clearly foreshadowing John Ireland's E minor sonata (published 1919), whose first movement has similarly a second subject in B♭ major. But an isolated experiment in modulation of this kind might mean little. Of far more significance is Byrd's frank abandonment of both the Dorian and the Phrygian modes. His 'minor' movements are written, with hardly an exception, in the Aeolian mode, both in its natural and transposed forms (i. e. D with one flat, or G with two flats, which are not left to the tender mercies of *Musica Ficta*, but inserted boldly as a key signature). In this practice he was followed by all the great madrigalists; here and there (as for instance in Morley's 'Hark Alleluia') you find a piece of deliberate modal writing; but the effect is that of an intentional archaism, and in this instance, one might add, the sentiment is curiously un-Phrygian. Compare the piece with, say, Palestrina's *Super flumina Babylonis,* and you see at once that the point of view is totally different.

The 'scalic' feeling of Wilbye's madrigal 'Draw on, sweet Night', with its sudden change from tonic major to tonic minor, has already been pointed out (see above, p. 62). Such instances are not hard to find in the English writers; another very striking one is Wilbye's 'Adieu, sweet Amaryllis', which (despite a single flat at the signature) is unmistakably in the key of G minor; but the last ten measures form a kind of epilogue which is no less unmistakably in the key of G major. Another proof of scale-feeling is to be found in the growing employment of harmonic sequence. Of this we give three striking instances from Byrd (Exx. 204–6). In these we can see plainly the transition from the old sense of modulation to the new; its use, that is to say, not to mark a point of repose, but to pass rapidly and easily from one tonality to another. In Ex. 206 the harmonic changes at measures 5 and 11 are remarkable, and the whole passage (clearly dictated by the character of the words) shows how freely Byrd was able to move about in such remote tonalities as F minor and A♭ major. The modulations are not so striking as some of those in Gesualdo, but they are more easily conducted, and more genuinely vocal in character.

Next, as to Melody. The reader who has marked and digested the rules of progression set forth on p. 30 might well be outraged at the sight of the leaps and plunges which the English composers expected their singers to make, had he not already been warned that the Englishmen were in many respects a law unto themselves. As usual, it is a case of distinguishing the artistic ideal in the technical method. What Palestrina and his school aimed at was perfect smoothness of progression and beauty of sound, whereas the Englishmen set greater store by vitality and boldness of outline. Mode, of course, goes by the board altogether; of what use to prate of ' authentic ' and ' plagal ' compass when we find Byrd, in ' Crowned with Flowers ', demanding from his tenor and contratenor such a range as that shown in Ex. 207 ? Nor is this angularity peculiar to Byrd, or to secular music; Exx. 208 to 216 from earlier composers like Tye, Whyte, and Taverner, as well as later men, illustrate a widespread partiality for this type of melodic curve, now soaring, now dipping, but always with the same unexpected rapid sweep. Ex. 209 from Robert Whyte shows the forbidden leap of a major ninth—a leap, moreover, which is continued in the same direction; Ex. 216 shows that the same writer is not afraid to treat the strictly forbidden interval of the major sixth with an equal want of ceremony. In Ex. 215 Wilbye takes the same interval sequentially in successive measures; indeed, all the Englishmen use it when-ever they have a mind to do so. In the Roman school, nevertheless, its prohibition is of all the rules, perhaps, the one that is most seldom infringed. Exx. 211 and 212 from Taverner illustrate not only the bold undulations beloved of that composer, but his fond-ness for the sequential organization of melody, a device invented, apparently, by Brumel, with whose work Taverner was doubtless acquainted. Ex. 213 also illustrates this propensity, and a good many other things, too; indeed, it is one of the most remarkable passages in the whole of sixteenth-century music. First of all there is the persistently sequential character of the melody as a whole; then there is the way in which the $\frac{3}{1}$ measures are telescoped successively by a $\frac{4}{2}$ rhythm and then by a $\frac{5}{2}$; finally, there is the astonishing emptiness and hollowness of timbre, the soprano and bass alone being in action, while at one point, it will be noticed, they are a clear three octaves apart. The effect, moreover, is cumulative, for the passage quoted is merely the climax of a long stretch of two-part writing which is started by contratenor and second bass, then taken up by alto and tenor, and finally by soprano and first bass as here shown, the breach being thus continually widened. Such an experiment could only have been conceived by a mind of singular daring and originality.

Many features of great harmonic interest are likewise to be found in the English composers. They may be classified roughly under four heads:

1. Greater freedom in the use of accented passing notes.
2. More varied methods of resolving discord.
3. More experimental formation of cadence.
4. A preference for the harsher forms of discord, especially for what are called 'false relationships'.

A few examples have been chosen to illustrate each of these in turn, and the following points are worth attention:

1. *Passing Notes.*

In the school of Palestrina, as we saw, accented passing notes are by no means infrequent, but they are only employed, as a rule, on the weak beats of the measure. The English composers frequently disregard this metrical restriction; they employ accented passing notes generally with greater freedom, and employ them without hesitation on the strong beats of the measure. In Exx. 217 and 218, both from Tye, we see the discordant interval of the fourth thus sounded without preparation on the first beat of the measure; Exx. 219 and 220, from Orlando Gibbons, show a similar use of the augmented fifth; in Ex. 221, from Byrd, we find in the first measure the chord of the dominant seventh; in the third, that of the diminished triad; in both places, it will be noticed, the chords arise naturally from the progression of the parts, and are created at a strong beat of the measure (the signature ₵ instead of C is here clearly a piece of carelessness on Byrd's part). In Exx. 222-5 the passing notes create an even stronger discord.

In this place, too (though it is not strictly relevant to the heading of the paragraph), it is convenient to point out two other harmonic peculiarities. The first (Ex. 226) is a figure to be found very frequently in Byrd, and it would seem to imply a recognition of the chord of the dominant seventh as a self-subsisting chord, for the seventh is approached freely, though it is not much emphasized. The second (Exx. 227 and 228), from Wilbye, is more difficult to classify. Dr. Fellowes regards it as a conscious employment of the chord known to modern theorists as that of the 'added sixth'; the present writer inclines to regard it rather as an unusual type of appoggiatura, in which the introductory note has somehow become detached from the note it prepares, and found its way into the preceding beat.

2. *Ornamental Forms of Resolving Discord.*

In addition to the forms of resolution mentioned in Chap. V, the following methods are employed, with varying degrees of frequency, by composers of the English school :

A. The suspended note may fall a fifth and then rise a fourth to the note of resolution (Exx. 229, 231).

B. It may fall a fourth and then rise a third (Ex. 231).

C. It may fall a third and then rise a second (rare: Ex. 230).

D. It may rise a second and then fall a third (Exx. 232, 233).

N.B.—In A, B, and C the intervening note reached by the fall must form a consonance with the remaining part or parts. Such resolutions as those shown in Exx. 235 and 236 are not to be found. The form D is a particular favourite of Tye, in whose work it occurs so frequently (in the manner shown at Ex. 232) as to be a positive mannerism. In Ex. 234 the two forms A and D are shown in combination, except that the F in the upper part is a concord and not a suspended discord, the G being a free passing note. The process, however, is clearly analogous. The passage may serve as a reminder that not only suspended discords but 'changing notes' are treated with greater freedom by the English composers than by the Flemish or Italian. Exx. 237–9 show two distinct varieties; but such instances are not easy to find, and there is no reason why a student should go out of his way to imitate them in his own writing.

It was given as a rule above (p. 39) that the preparation, creation, and resolution of discord should take place on successive beats, three beats thus being required for the whole process. The duration of the beat depends, of course, on the time-signature: in ₵ it is the minim, in C the crotchet; in O and Φ it may be the minim, but is usually the semibreve; in ⊙ and C it is the minim. Occasionally (though really very seldom), the English writers allow the creation and resolution of a discord to take place within the duration of a single beat. In Ex. 240, for instance (sign C), the process is completed within a crotchet beat; in Ex. 241 (sign C) within that of a minim. It is not recommended that a student should permit himself this rare licence, for it will tend to weaken his sense of metrical exactitude, and unless this is preserved, rhythmical freedom easily degenerates into confusion. Of course there is no reason why a modern composer should not throw metre overboard and write frankly in prose rhythm, if he wants to; but such a method is radically different from that of sixteenth-century counterpoint. To illustrate the extremely unpleasant effect produced by preparing a suspension on the strong beat and creating it on the next weak beat (and not vice versa), Ex. 242 is appended. Such a solecism is very rarely to be found; it serves to show how important it is that metrical strictness should persist and make itself felt through all the rhythmic independence of the individual parts.

3. Cadence.

The forms of cadence to be found in the English writers are less stereotyped than those of composers like Lasso or Vittoria. These experiments are not always successful; sometimes a composer spoils a fine composition by ending with a tentative and unsatisfying cadence that leaves no sense of finality. A case in point is the splendid 'Hierusalem, convertere ad Dominum', from Tallis's *Lamentations*—a work whose tragic and sombre intensity of conviction is hardly reached by any other music of this period, or indeed of any period. Yet the effect of all that has gone before is marred by the hesitation in the bass as it proceeds to the final cadence (see the penultimate measure of Ex. 243). The other cadences in the *Lamentations* are masterly; Ex. 244 is a particularly beautiful one, the secret of which is the juxtaposition of the sharpened and flattened seventh (C♮ and C♯). Ex. 245, from Byrd's *Gradualia*, is clearly related to it, and though wholly different in spirit, is no less beautiful. Byrd was a pupil of Tallis, and one might easily suppose that he borrowed the idea from his master. The real inventor of it, however, would seem once again to be the enterprising Taverner, for in Ex. 246 (quoted in Morley's *Plaine and Easie Introduction*) we find all its essential features, though the details are differently contrived. Morley's comments are of interest:

'The close in the counter (is) both naught and stale. . . . This point when the lesson was made being a new fashion was admitted for the raritie . . . but nowadays it is grown in such common use as divers will make no scruple to use it in few parts, whereas it might well enough be left out, though it be very usuall with our Organists.'

Evidently the *cliché* was not unknown, even in those days. The 'Organists', however, have ceased from troubling (at least, those particular ones have), and we of to-day can surrender to the spell of the cadence without the necessity of reminding ourselves that it was once common property. Echoes of it are to be found at the end of Purcell's 'Full Fathom Five'. Ex. 247 is a quite experimental 'feminine' cadence from Byrd; Ex. 248 (also quite experimental) is from Taverner; in this cadence the bass, instead of approaching the final by the interval of the fourth or fifth, or by the descent of one degree, comes up to it by a stepwise ascent—a most unusual progression at a close, which can be paralleled, however, from Palestrina (Ex. 249). The Taverner passage, despite the bold sustention of the B and D by the alto voices in the last measure but two, is not wholly convincing, but the Palestrina cadence is quite perfect— another instance of the exquisite judgement that enables him to carry off a situation with which a less unerring genius is not quite able to cope. Once more, the secret of it is the tact with which the E♮ and the E♭ are played off against one another.

Two concluding instances are given from Byrd. In Ex. 250 there is an unusual treatment of the 'changing note' formula, the second note being treated not as a passing note, but as the resolution of a prepared discord, the discord and its resolution occurring within the space of a single beat; while to get his harmony right Byrd does not hesitate to make his tenor sing E♮, although there is an E♭ in the key signature, and although the E, in any case, coming between D and D, would normally be sung as E♭ in accordance with the customs of *Musica Ficta*. The cadence sounds so natural and convincing that one does not realize its novel and daring character until one examines it in detail. Ex. 251 is given to show the free use of the dominant seventh (B♭) at the final cadence. Byrd uses a similar formula freely (cf. Ex. 225), but not as a rule in such an emphatic position. The cadential formula shown in Ex. 222, however, where the seventh (G) is treated as an ordinary changing note, is of constant occurrence.

4. *General Characteristics of Harmony.*

From instances already given the student will have seen that the tendency of the English school in general is towards a bolder and more rugged type of harmony than foreign composers permitted themselves. A few more such instances may be cited. In Ex. 252

the accented passing note (E♭) in the alto is taken in orthodox fashion on a weak beat of the measure, but its double clash against the D of the cantus and the B of the tenor creates a very aggressive dissonance. Ex. 253 is similar in character; the combination of D, A, E, B, and G into a single chord is remarkable even for Byrd. In Ex. 254, by using an upward-resolving suspension in the bass, the same composer manages to employ the notes E, F, A, and C♯ in combination. The bass, it will be seen, after touching D goes down to B♭, the treatment of the suspended note being thus in strict conformity with English principles, except that the ultimate resolution is by the fall of an augmented second—C♯ to B♭. But so marked a characteristic of English composition is better realized by a perusal of the music in long stretches than by examining a few singular instances. Its harmony in general has a rough tang, which may not suit every one, but is extremely palatable to those who have once acquired a taste for it.

There is, however, one peculiar manifestation of it which cannot be overlooked, and that is the fondness of these writers for what we call false relationships. Dr. Walker, in his *History of Music in England*, has devoted a considerable part of one chapter to this subject, and has collected some curious instances; it is therefore not necessary to treat it here at any great length. The origin of the practice is to be found in the rules of *Musica Ficta*; if the student will turn to p. 11 and note what is there said under heading (6) and then examine Exx. 255–8, he will see that the progression of the parts is quite logical.

It should be added, too, that there was a general tendency on the part of singers at this period, in scale passages, to sharpen the seventh going up and to flatten it coming down, so that fairly close juxtapositions of B♮ and B♭, C♮ and C♯, and so on, would inevitably occur quite often, whether specifically intended by the composer or not. But the Englishmen went much further than the foreign composers, for they positively went out of their way to bring about these clashes in a single chord. To us to-day it seems a perfectly simple and natural proceeding; it is merely honouring the claims of the intellect in preference to those of the senses—a sacrifice which a composer of the highest order must always be ready to make. But our fathers and grandfathers were sadly perplexed at some of the things they found, and no wonder. Mendelssohn never played them such pranks: who were Tallis and Gibbons and these other old fogies, that they should dare put such things on paper, and call it harmony? So, armed with a pen mightier than any sword, the editors with one consent began to edit; timely suppressions and judicious emendations were the order of the day, until finally Tallis, Byrd, & Co. emerged with their hair curled and their beards trimmed, quite presentable, quite fit for the best Victorian society —but curiously unlike their real selves. The examples already quoted will show the type of passage that thus caused our ancestors to stumble. Once the contrapuntal explanation is grasped, the composer's intention becomes perfectly clear, and further comment is unnecessary.

Finally, as to Rhythm. Despite the many individual features that mark the melody and the harmony of the English composers, it is above all by their rhythm that they live. They have no monopoly of rhythmic freedom, for all the music of the period, as we have seen, is rhythmically far in advance of any music that has been written since. Harmony itself, apart from the simplest concords, was merely a by-product of rhythmical experiment; the whole of sixteenth-century texture is essentially an interweaving of independent rhythms, and not (as commonly said) a combination of melodies. This volume has missed its aim entirely if it has failed to make it clear to the student that counterpoint *is* rhythm, and very little else.

It is none the less true that the peculiar glory of the Englishmen is their mastery of rhythmic device. They seem to have an inexhaustible wealth of enterprise and resource, and it would take nothing less than a volume to do justice to this aspect of their technique. Some examples have already been given (see Chap. III), but one or two more may fitly serve to conclude this chapter, and so bring these pages to a close. The example from Byrd (Ex. 259) has been chosen to illustrate his fondness for rhythmical combination within a triple measure. 'Triple measure' is, perhaps, a misnomer, for of the five parts only one bears the genuine triple-time signature (Φ), the others all bearing the sign C, which stands for what we should call compound duple time. Whether this variation is an oversight on Byrd's part, or whether it is intentional, is of no moment. The essential feature of the madrigal is the persistent conflict of the three-one and the six-two accentuations; a conflict, moreover, which is never allowed to become mechanical—note, for instance, the seventh and eighth measures, where the soprano breaks in with quite an independent rhythm of its own, the two measures together resolving into $\frac{4}{2} + \frac{3}{2} + \frac{5}{2}$. At the same time, the alto complicates matters by contradicting the accents of the soprano in every possible place. The basic idea of the work, none the less, is the contrast of the three-one (♩♩ ♩♩ ♩♩) and the six-two (♩♩♩ ♩♩♩).

It is a favourite device of Byrd's, and the present writer had much hesitation in deciding which of his pieces to select for the illustration of it; 'My Mind to me a Kingdom is', and 'Though Amaryllis dance in green' were abandoned with very great reluctance, for they show an equally consummate mastery. Both are to be found in Dr. Fellowes's edition of the *Psalms, Sonnets, and Songs* of 1588, and every student should make a point of reading and if possible hearing them for himself. If the members of a class would put their heads together and sing them, they would really learn more about counterpoint in half-an-hour than any master could teach them in a month. For another example, in this volume, the reader may turn to the short extract from 'Arise, Lord' (Ex. 205), quoted to illustrate quite a different aspect of Byrd's technique, but equally relevant in this place. The signature here is C, but it will be found on analysis that the rhythm of the top part is a regular $\frac{6}{4}$, that of the other parts an equally regular $\frac{3}{2}$.

Our last two examples are both from the pen of Mr. Thomas Morley—immortal author of the *Plaine and Easie Introduction to Practical Harmony*, the only musical text-book ever written to be read for its own sake, as one reads a novel. As a composer of madrigals, Morley is perhaps the least of his peers: he has not the passion of Weelkes, the profundity of Gibbons, or the radiant imagination of Wilbye. But though not himself the greatest in an age of greatness, he is yet one of its most characteristic figures, and his best work is full of a gusto and vivacity that mark him out as a chosen representative of the Comic Spirit in music. His technique he learnt from Byrd, and to say that the pupil was worthy of the master is both to give him his bare due and to pay him the highest compliment his heart could desire. In sheer exuberance of rhythm Morley has never been surpassed; there are so many passages in our madrigalists which take one's breath away that one must needs hesitate to speak in superlatives; but if driven to an offhand choice, the writer would be inclined to name 'Arise, get up, my Dear' as the most exhilarating *tour de force* in the whole collection. 'Whither away so fast' is not far behind, and with two of the most exciting episodes from this pair of canzonets, our somewhat lengthy list of illustrations comes to a close. The reader must imagine both of them sung at racing speed, lightly and breezily, yet with a resolute enforcement of every stress and counterstress that may serve to darken the plot and complicate the issue. Analysis, after what has been said before, would be pedantry; three voices only are employed; all the student has to do is to see how it is done, and then go and do it himself.

There is always danger in the attempt to deal cursorily with a large subject; however great one's vigilance, there is always the chance that something vital may be omitted in the process of summarization. The foregoing remarks, it is hoped, may give the student some idea of the lines on which technical examination must proceed, before we can form a just critical estimate of our national achievements in the sixteenth century. More than that they are not intended to do. It may, perhaps, be added that materials for such a critique have hitherto been lacking; vast quantities of important works have been buried away in part books, and even where the work of scoring and publication has been carried out, the result has been too often untrustworthy. Now, things have been changed; scholars like Dr. Fellowes, Mr. Arkwright, Mr. Barclay Squire, Dr. Terry (to name no others) have been hard at work, and the preparation and issue of both the sacred and the secular work has been taken in hand; of the latter, indeed, the more important half has already been published. A man, however, may not be his own judge, and the ultimate verdict on the Tudor composers will not depend on our national predilections, but on the consensus of European opinion. But we must see to it that that opinion is based on adequate research and thorough knowledge of the period under review; we must raise our voice in no uncertain protest against any critic who attempts to pass judgement on a hasty or partial survey of the material which our scholars have placed at his disposal. German critics have pulled our nose in the past; there seems every likelihood that French critics will try to do so in the future. The only reply is to pull theirs harder, but the attempt will be ineffective unless we are very sure of ourselves and our knowledge. That knowledge must be extensive and thorough, and it must be a knowledge of their work as well as ours. Thus armed, we can feel secure. We need not expect the judgement of the world to coincide with our own, but we can insist that judgement be passed only by competent observers, and that its foundations rest on a bedrock of reason and justice.

EXAMPLES

EXAMPLES.

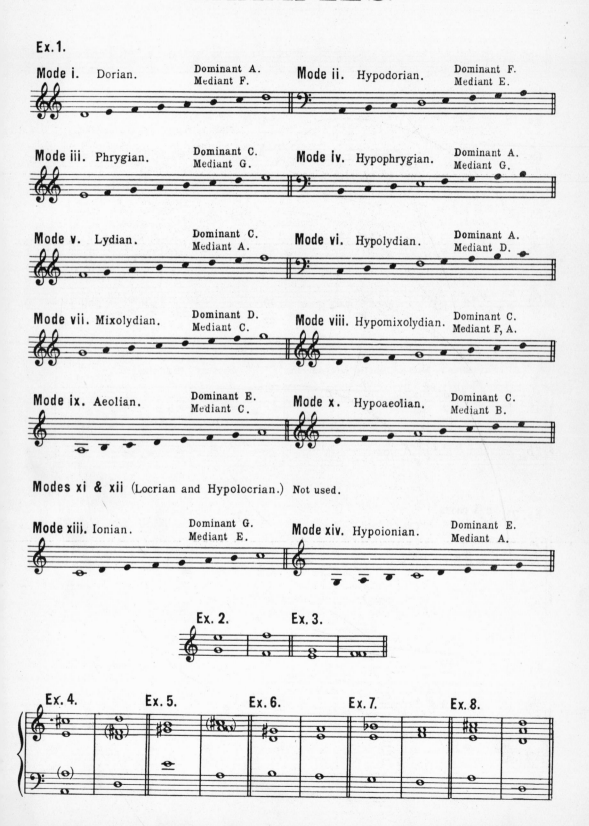

Ex. 1.

Mode i. Dorian. — Dominant A. Mediant F.

Mode ii. Hypodorian. — Dominant F. Mediant E.

Mode iii. Phrygian. — Dominant C. Mediant G.

Mode iv. Hypophrygian. — Dominant A. Mediant G.

Mode v. Lydian. — Dominant C. Mediant A.

Mode vi. Hypolydian. — Dominant A. Mediant D.

Mode vii. Mixolydian. — Dominant D. Mediant C.

Mode viii. Hypomixolydian. — Dominant C. Mediant F, A.

Mode ix. Aeolian. — Dominant E. Mediant C.

Mode x. Hypoaeolian. — Dominant C. Mediant B.

Modes xi & xii (Locrian and Hypolocrian.) Not used.

Mode xiii. Ionian. — Dominant G. Mediant E.

Mode xiv. Hypoionian. — Dominant E. Mediant A.

Ex. 2.   **Ex. 3.**

Ex. 4.   **Ex. 5.**   **Ex. 6.**   **Ex. 7.**   **Ex. 8.**

Ex. 9.   Ex. 10.   Ex. 11.   Ex. 12.   Ex. 13.   Ex. 14.

Ex. 15. In 2 parts.
Orlando Lasso, Ps: Pen: VII.

Ex. 16. In 2 parts.
Idem, Magn. op. mus., № 8.

Ex. 17. In 3 parts.
Palestrina, Missa, *Lauda Sion*, (Benedictus).

Ex. 18. In 3 parts.
Croce, Missa Tertii Toni, (Credo).

Ex. 19. In 3 parts
Palestrina, Missa Quarta. (Benedictus).

Ex. 20. In 4 parts.
Ibidem. (Sanctus)

Ex. 21. In 4 parts.
Palestrina, Missa, *Iste Confessor*,
(Christe Eleison).

Ex. 22. In 5 parts.
Palestrina, Missa, *Regina Coeli*,
(Sanctus).

Ex. 23. In 6 parts.
Palestrina, Missa, *Assumpta est Maria*,
Agnus Dei I.

Ex. 24. Palestrina, *Missa Brevis* (Credo).
Sectional Cadence.

Ex. 25. Ibidem.
Final Cadence.

Ex. 26.
"Phrygian" Cadence.
2 parts.

Ex. 27.
3 parts.

Ex. 28.
4 parts.

Ex. 29. In 2 parts.
Orlando Lasso, *Oculus non Vidit*.

Ex. 30. In 3 parts.
Vittoria, Missa Quarti Toni
(Benedictus).

Ex. 31. In 4 parts.
Vittoria, *O vos omnes*.

Ex. 32. Plagal cadence in 3 parts.
Palestrina, Missa Brevis
(Benedictus).

Ex. 33. In 4 parts.
Ibidem (Credo).

Ex. 34. In 5 parts.
Ibidem (Agnus Dei).

&c.

Ex. 35. Vittoria, *O Magnum Mysterium*.

Ex. 36. *Interrupted Cadence* (Form I).
Palestrina, *Gaudent in Coelis*.

Ex. 37. (Form II).
Idem, Missa, *Regina Coeli*.
(Gloria).

&c.

&c.

Gau-dent in coe _____ (lis)

Ex. 38.

Ex. 39. Palestrina, *Stabat Mater.*

Sta - bat ma - ter do - lo - ro - sa, jux - ta cru - cem la - cri - mo - sa

Ex. 39ª

Sta - bat ma - ter do - lo - ro - sa jux - ta cru - cem la - cri - mo - sa

Ex. 40. Ibidem.

Fac ut te - cum lu - ge - am, fac ut ar - de - at cor me - um, in a -

man - do Chris - tum De - um, ut si - bi com - pla - ce - am

Ex. 40ª (The note-values reduced for the purpose of illustration to their approximate

Fac ut te - cum lu - ge - am, fac ut ar - de - at cor me - um, in a -

modern equivalent).

man - do Chris - tum De - um ut si - bi com - pla - ce - am

Ex. 41. Morales, *Officium Defunctorum,* Lectio III.

ma - nus tu - - ae fe - ce - - runt me

Ex. 42. Orlando Lasso, *Neue Teutsche Lieder,* II, 8.

es sind doch se - lig al - le - die, al - le die, es sind doch se - lig

al - le die, in rech - tem glau - ben wan - deln hie

Ex. 43. Byrd, "O God which art most merciful."

ac - cor-ding to the mul - ti - tude of Thy com-pas-si-ons seen

Ex. 44. Morley, 3-part canzonet.

Blow, she - pherd, blow, blow your pipes with glee re - sound - - ing

Ex. 45. Bertani, "Ch'ami la Vita" [from "Arion"]

ch'a - mi la vi - ta mia nel · tuo bel no - - me

Ex. 46. Morley, "Still it frieth."

yet my heart ne-ver di - eth, my heart ne-ver di - eth, my heart ne-ver di - - eth.

Ex. 47. Idem, "Why sit I here complaining?"

hence a - way, com - fort, in vain — thou dost ease we, com - fort in vain thou

Ex. 48. Pevernage, "Recherche qui voudra."

Pour l'ombre et pour la soif, pour l'ombre et pour la soif, du - rant les grand chaleurs, pour

Ex. 49. Idem, "Fais que je vive."

mè - re des mal-heu-reux, mè-re des mal-heu-reux, mè - re des mal-heu-reux,

8

Ex. 50.

Sta - bat ma-ter do - lo - ro - sa   fac, ut te - cum lu-ge-am, fac, ut ar -

Ex. 51. Palestrina, *Missa Papae Marcelli.*

Ky - ri - e,e lei - - - - - - son, e

-lei - - - - - - - - - - son.

Ex. 52. Idem, Missa, *Assumpta Est Maria.*

Qui ve - - - - - - - - - nit   in

no - mi - ne Do - - - - - - - - - mi - ni, Qui

Ex. 53. *Ibidem.*

Et   in spi - ri-tum Sanc - tum Do - mi-num, et vi-vi-fi - can-tem, Qui

ex Pa - tre Fi - li - o - - que pro - ce - dit. Qui cum

Ex. 54. Brumel, Missa, *De Beata Virgine.*

Ky - ri - e, e - lei - - - - son, e - lei - -

- - son, Ky - - ri - e, e - lei - son

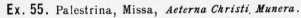

Ex. 55. Palestrina, Missa, *Aeterna Christi. Munera*.

Ex. 56. Palestrina, *Mori quasi il mio core*.

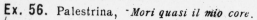

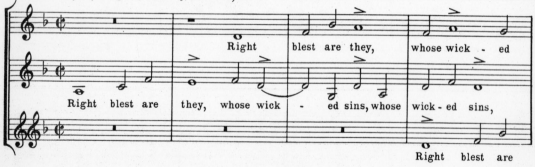

Ex. 57. Byrd, *Songs of Sundry Natures*, N⁰ 2.

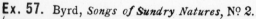

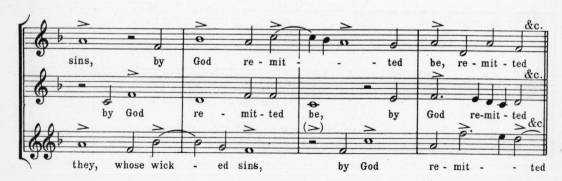

Ex. 58. Ibidem No 16.

Ex. 59. Idem Four-part Mass.

Ex. 60. Wilbye, "Down in a Valley."

Ex. 61.

Ex. 61ª.

Ex. 62. Bugsworthy, Conceits and Vapours, № 10001.

Ex. 63. Ibidem, № 10002.

Ex. 64. Palestrina, Missa, *Assumpta est Maria*, (Kyrie I). **Ex. 65.** Ibidem,(Agnus Dei I).

Ex. 66. Ibidem (Christe Eleison). **Ex. 67.** Ibidem. **Ex. 68.** Vittoria, *Veni Creator*.

Ex. 69. Palestrina, Missa, *Regina Cœli*, (Credo). **Ex. 70.** Ibidem, (Benedictus).

Ex. 71. (Faulty progression). **Ex. 72.** Palestrina, Missa, *Assumpta est Maria* (Benedictus).

Ex. 73. Ibidem. **Ex. 74.** Ibidem,(Christe Eleison).

Ex. 75. Byrd, "I thought that Love". **Ex. 76.** Idem, "Have Mercy upon me".

Ex. 90. Byrd, *Sacerdotes Domini.*

Ex. 91. Palestrina, *Hodie Christus natus est.*
(quick time; original signature φ 3/2).

Ex. 92. Palestrina, *Tollite jugum.*
(fairly slow time; signature φ).

Ex. 93. Byrd, "I thought that Love".
(quick time; signature ℂ).

Ex. 94. Idem, 5-part Mass.

Ex. 95. Brumel, Missa, *De beata Virgine* (Gloria).

Ex. 96. John Farmer, 4-part madrigal,
"Take Time whilst Time doth last".

Ex. 97. Palestrina, *Missa Brevis*
(Agnus Dei I).

Ex. 98. Palestrina, Lamentations.
(Lectio I, Fer. VI).

Ex. 99. Morales,
Lamentabatur Jacob.

Ex. 100. Idem,
Magnificat viii Toni.

Ex. 101. Palestrina, Missa, *Assumpta est Maria*, (Benedictus).

Ex. 102. (Harmonic skeleton).

Ex. 103. Idem, *Tollite jugum*.

Ex. 104. Idem, Missa, *Assumpta est Maria* (Osanna).

Ex 105. Idem, *Gaudent in Cœlis*.

Ex 106. Byrd, "O you that hear this Voice".

Ex. 107. Palestrina, *Lauda Sion*.

Ex. 108. P. de la Rue, Missa, *Ave Maria* (Osanna).

Ex. 109. **Ex. 110.** **Ex. 111.** **Ex. 112.**
Simple form of resolution.   Ornamental forms of resolution.

Ex. 113. **Ex. 114.** **Ex. 115.**

Ex.116. Guerrero, *O Domine Jesu Christe.*

Ex.117. Palestrina, Missa, *Assumpta est Maria* (Agnus Dei). (Treatment of the $\frac{6}{4}$ chord as a double suspension).

Ex.118. Palestrina, *Missa Brevis* (Agnus Dei II). Double suspension of the 3rd as a $\frac{9}{7}$ chord.

Ex. 119. Palestrina, Missa, *Aeterna Christi Munera*. Double suspension of the 4th (Christe Eleison).

Ex. 120. *Missa de Feria*, Agnus Dei I. Another instance from Palestrina.

Ex. 121. Palestrina, Missa, *De Beata Virgine* (Credo). Double suspension of the 5th.

Ex. 122. *Missa Papae Marcelli*, (Kyrie). Another instance from Palestrina.

Ex. 123. *Missa Brevis* (Credo). Another instance from Palestrina

Ex.124. Byrd, 5-part Mass (Treatment of the $\frac{6}{4}$ chord as a double suspension of the 6th).

Ex.125. Palestrina, *Missa de Feria*, (Kyrie I). Double suspension of the 6th.

Ex.126. Palestrina, Missa, *Jam Christus Astra* (Credo). Double suspension of the 6th as a $\frac{9}{4}$ chord, followed by that of the 3rd as a $\frac{7}{5}$ chord.

Ex.127. Palestrina, Madrigals, Bk. II, No 18. (Suspension of a 3-part chord; (cf Ex.86)

Ex.128. Byrd, 5-part Mass (Christe Eleison).

18

Ex. 144. Palestrina, *O Bone Jesu.*

Ex. 145. Orlando Lasso, Ps. Pen. II.

Ex. 146. Palestrina, Lamentations (Lectio I).

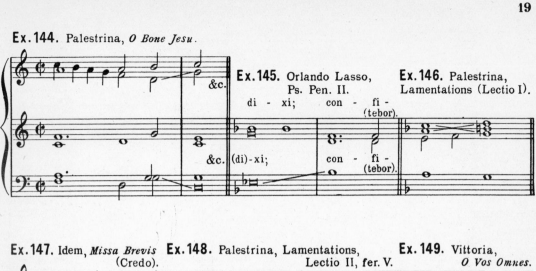

Ex. 147. Idem, *Missa Brevis* (Credo).

Ex. 148. Palestrina, Lamentations, Lectio II, fer. V.

Ex. 149. Vittoria, *O Vos Omnes.*

Ex. 150. Ibidem.

Ex. 151. Idem, *Missa Pro Defunctis* (Credo).

Ex. 152. A. Gabrieli, Missa Brevis (Agnus Dei).

Ex. 153. Aichinger, *Lauda anima mea.*

Ex. 154. Palestrina, *Salvator Mundi.*

Ex. 155. Orlando Lasso, *Missa viii Toni* (Gloria).

Ex. 156. Vittoria, *O vos omnes.*

20

Ex.158. Marenzio, *Magnum haereditatis mysterium.*

Ex.159. Orlando Lasso, *Missa V vocum.*

Ex. 160. Giaches de Wert, "Chi salira per me."

Ex.161. Marenzio, *Misit Rex Ministros.*

Ex.162. Tallis, *O Sacrum Convivium.*

Ex.163. Orlando Lasso, Missa, *In Die Tribulationis.* (Kyrie)

Ex.164. Soriano, Missa, *Nos autem gloriari.* (Christe eleison)

Ex.165. Hassler, *Missa Tertia IV Vocum.*

Ex.166. Vittoria, Missa, *Trahe me post te.*

Ex.167. Tallis, *Derelinquit impius.*

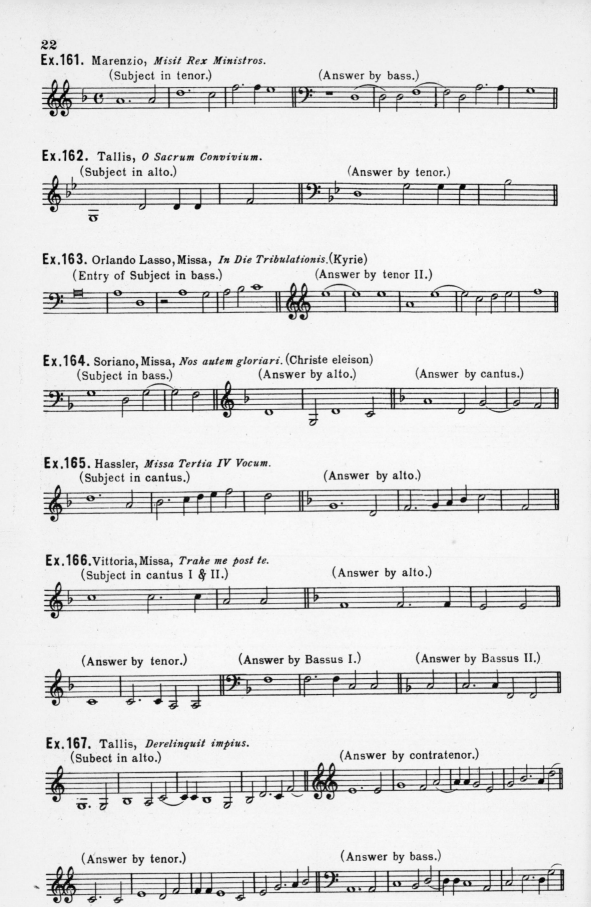

Ex. 168. Palestrina, Missa, *Veni Sponsa Christi*. (Sanctus.)

Ex. 169. Idem, *Missa de Feria*. (Kyrie II.)

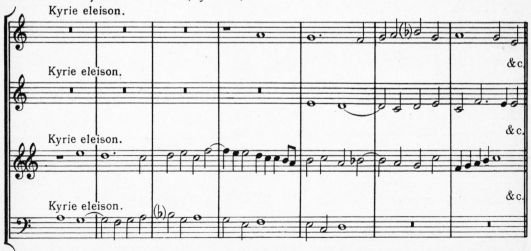

Ex.170. Palestrina, *Terra Tremuit.*

Ex.171. Ibidem (the same entries inverted at the 12th by altus and bassus)

Ex.172. Marenzio, *Cum Jucunditate.*

Ex.173. Ibidem, (the same entries inverted by cantus and tenor at the 12ᵗʰ, changing to the 8ᵗʰ)

Ex.174. Idem, *Te Deum Patrem*. (inversion at the 10ᵗʰ, changing to the 8ᵗʰ)

Ex.175. Idem, *Princeps gloriosissime.*

Inversion by C. and A. at the 9th changing to the 8th

CANTUS.　　　(Subject in T and B)

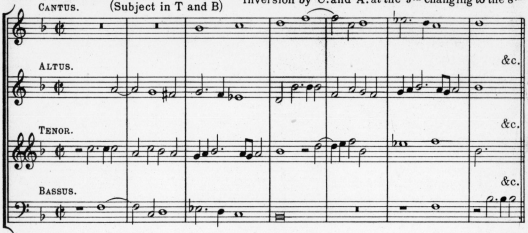

ALTUS.

&c.

TENOR.

&c.

BASSUS.

&c.

Ex.176. Idem, *Iste est Joannes.* Triple Counterpoint.

Themes.

Order.

Ex.177. Sweelinck, "Poi che non voleté" (Answer by inversion.)

Ex.178. Marenzio, *Te Deum Patrem* (Answer by inversion)

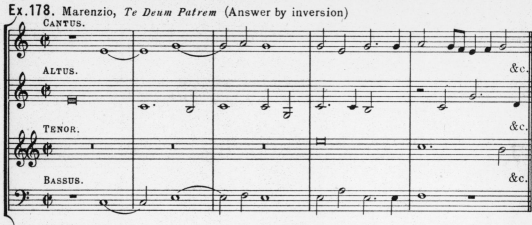

Ex.179. Idem, *Hodie Completi Sunt.*

(Answer by inversion in two parts)

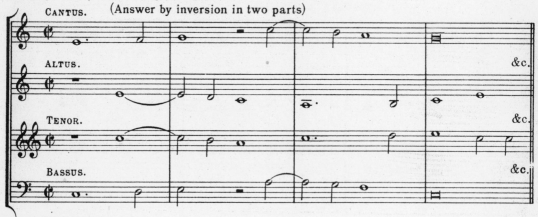

Ex.180. Palestrina, *Missa ad Fugam* (Kyrie)

Ex.181. Ibidem (Credo)

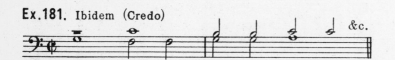

Ex.182. Ibidem, (Benedictus)

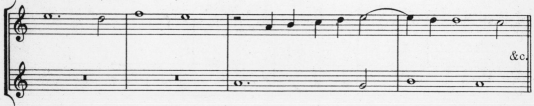

Ex.183. Palestrina, *Missa Brevis.*

Canon two in one at the unison.
Agnus Dei &c.

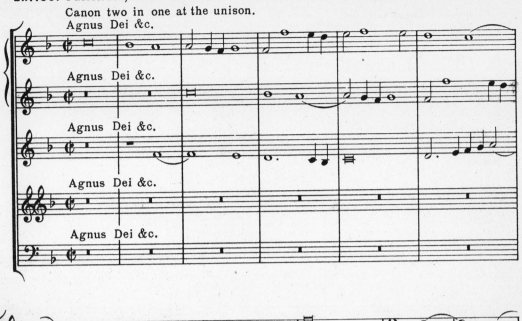

Ex.184. Palestrina, Missa, *Sacerdotes Domini* (Sanctus)

Ex. 185. Byrd, *Diliges Dominum Deum.*
Canon Eight in Four, *per Recte et Retro.*

&c.

Ex. 186. Ibidem (the last six measures).

Ex. 187.

Ve - ni, Spon - sa Chris ti, Ac - ci - pe Co - ro - nam,

quam ti - bi do - mi - nus prae pa - ra - vit in ae - ter - nam.

Ex. 188.   Ex. 189.

Ex. 190.   Ex. 191.

Ex. 192. Palestrina, Motet, *Veni Sponsa Christi.*

CANTAS.

Ve - ni, Spon - sa Chris - - - -

ALTUS.

Ve - ni, Spon - sa Chris - - - -

TENOR.

Ve -

BASSUS.

- ti

- ti

- ni, Spon - sa Chris - - - - ti

Ve - ni, Spon - sa Chris - - - ti

Do - mi - nus

prae - pa - ra-vit in   ae - ter - num

prae - pa - ra-vit in ____ ae - ter -

prae - pa - ra-vit in

- num

prae - pa - ra-vit in ____ ae - ter - num

ae - ter - num

Ex.193. Palestrina, Motet, *Tu es Petrus* (first section).

Ex.194. Palestrina *O Bone Jesu.*

O Bo - ne Je - - su, Mi - se - re - re no - -

bis qui - a tu cre - as - ti nos, tu re - de -

mis - ti nos San -gui - ne tu - o pre - ti - o -sis - - - si - mo.

Ex.195. Palestrina, Missa, *Aeterna Christi Munera.* **Ex.195ª** Melody in Credo.
Melody in Kyrie. &c.

Ex.195ᵇ Melody in Sanctus.
&c.

Ex.195ᶜ Melody in Agnus Dei I. **Ex.195ᵈ** Melody in Agnus Dei II.

Ex.196. Gesualdo,"Ardo per te." **Ex.197.** Idem, "Ardita Zanzaretta"

&c.

Ex.198. Idem, (from the bass part of "Gia piansi.")

Ex.199. Orlando Lasso, "Hor qui son."

Ex.200. Idem, "se si alto pon gir."

Ex.201. "Hora per far."

Ex.202. Wilbye, "Thou art but young thou says't."

And thou shalt wish (but wishes all shall fail thee) and thou shalt wish (but wi-shes all shall fail thee)&c

Ex.203. Wilbye, Madrigal, "Draw on, Sweet Night."

Draw on, sweet night draw on sweet night

Draw on sweet night,

Draw on sweet night, best friend un-to those cares

Draw on sweet night, best friend un-to those

40

45

50

un-to thee I con-se-crate it whol - ly: Sweet night draw on &c.

I con-se-crate it whol - ly: Sweet

That un-to thee I con-se-crate it wholly: Sweet night draw on

un-to thee to thee I con-se-crate it wholly:

- ly, _____ it whol - ly: Sweet night draw on

I con - se-crate it whol - ly:

Ex. 204. Byrd, *Sacerdotes Domini.*

&c.

Ex. 205. Idem, "Arise Lord into Thy Rest."

Re-joice re-joice re-joice re-joice re-joice re-joice, and let &c.

re-joice re-joice &c.

(re)-joice re-joice re-joice &c. and let &c.

(re)- joice re-joice re-joice &c. and let the saints re(joice

re-joice re - joice &c. and let &c.

Ex. 206. Idem, "Come, woeful Orpheus."

of   sou - rest   sharps   and   un - couth   flats,

and   un - couth   flats   make   choice,   make   choice.

Ex. 207.
(Contratenor)   (Tenor)

Ex. 208. Tye, *Amavit.*   &c.

Ex. 209. Whyte, *Deus Misereatur.*   &c.

Ex. 210. Idem, *Tota pulcra es, amica mea.*   &c.

Ex. 211. Taverner, Missa, *Gloria tibi Trinitas* (Gloria).   &c.

Ex. 212. Ibidem, (Agnus Dei).   &c.

Ex. 213. Idem, Missa *Corona Spinea* (Pleni Sunt Coeli).

&c.

Ex. 228. Idem, "There where I saw."

Ex. 229. Byrd, *Aspice Domine.*

Ex. 230. Byrd, "Christ is Risen Again." (Part II)

Ex. 231. Whyte, "O Praise God in his holiness."

Ex. 232. Tye, Missa, *Euge Bone.* (Gloria)

Ex. 233. Ibidem.

Ex. 234. Whyte, *Deus Misereatur.*

Ex. 235.

Ex. 236.

Incorrect resolutions.

Ex. 237. Tallis, Mass (Benedictus).

Ex. 238. Ibidem.

Ex. 239. Byrd, "Lord in Thy wrath."

Ex. 240. Gibbons, "Dainty Fine Bird."

Ex. 241. Byrd, "Christ is Risen Again."

Ex. 242. Tye, Missa, *Euge Bone* (Credo)

Ex. 243. Tallis, Lamentations, Lectio I.

Ex. 244. Ibidem.

Ex. 245. Byrd, *Sacerdotes Domini.*

Ex. 246. Quoted by Morley from Taverner.

Ex. 247. Byrd, "But not too soon."

Ex. 248. Taverner, Missa, *Gloria tibi Trinitas* (Osanna).

Ex. 249. Palestrina, Lamentations Bk. I. Lectio III, Fer I.

Ex. 250. Byrd, "Mine eyes with Fervency."

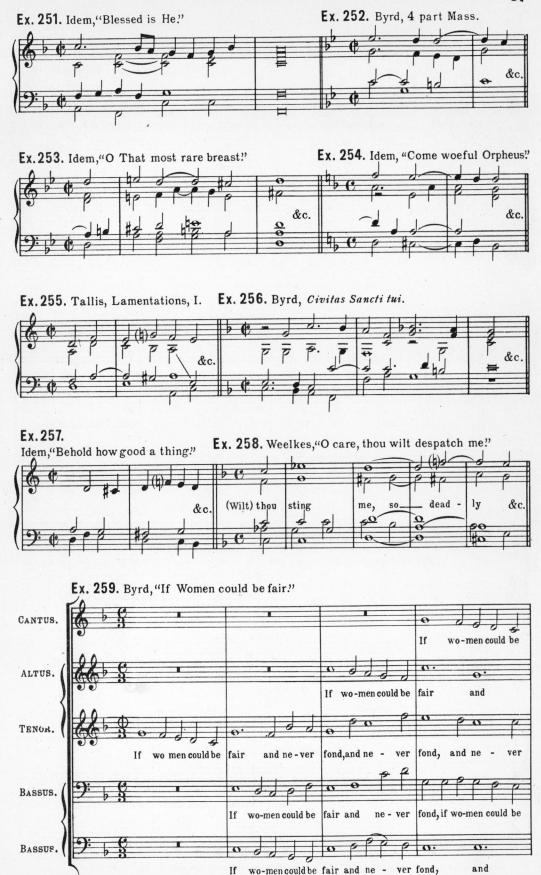

Ex. 251. Idem, "Blessed is He."

Ex. 252. Byrd, 4 part Mass.

Ex. 253. Idem, "O That most rare breast."

Ex. 254. Idem, "Come woeful Orpheus."

Ex. 255. Tallis, Lamentations, I.

Ex. 256. Byrd, *Civitas Sancti tui.*

Ex. 257. Idem, "Behold how good a thing."

Ex. 258. Weelkes, "O care, thou wilt despatch me."

Ex. 259. Byrd, "If Women could be fair."

Ex. 260. Morley, 3-part canzonets, N⁰ 7, "Whither away so fast?"

Ex. 261. Ibidem, № 20, "Arise get up my dear."